American Book Company's

MASTERING THE GEORGIA 4TH GRADE CRCT IN READING

ALIGNED TO THE GEORGIA PERFORMANCE STANDARDS (GPS)

Sara Hinton, Kristie Smith, Leah Ott, Lisa M. Cocca

Reviewer: Dr. Karen H. Michael

Project Coordinator: Zuzana Urbanek

Executive Editor: Dr. Frank J. Pintozzi

AMERICAN BOOK COMPANY

PO BOX 2638

WOODSTOCK, GEORGIA 30188-1383

Toll Free: 1 (888) 264-5877   Phone: 770-928-2834

Toll Free Fax: 1 (866) 827-3240

Web site: www.americanbookcompany.com

ACKNOWLEDGEMENTS

The authors would like to gratefully acknowledge the formatting contributions of Yvonne Benson and Marsha Torrens, as well as the graphics expertise of Charisse Johnson.

Many thanks go to Mallory Grantham for her editing contributions.

The authors express their appreciation to Dr. Karen Michael for her expert review of the content in this book.

Table of Contents

4R1a, f, h Inf

4R1b, d, e Inf

4R1g Inf

4LSV2a, b, c

Mastering the Georgia 4th Grade CRCT in Reading
Preface

Mastering the Georgia 4th Grade CRCT in Reading will help students who are learning or reviewing the GPS standards for the Reading sections of the **Georgia 4th Grade CRCT in Reading**. The materials in this book are based on the GPS standards as published by the Georgia Department of Education. This book is written to the grade 4 level, corresponding to approximately 650L to 850L on the Lexile text measure scale.

This book contains several sections:

1) General information about the book itself

2) A diagnostic test

3) An evaluation chart

4) Twelve chapters that teach the concepts and skills needed for test readiness

5) Two practice tests

Standards are posted at the beginning of each chapter, in the diagnostic and practice tests, and in a chart included in the answer manual.

We welcome your comments and suggestions. Please contact us at

American Book Company
PO Box 2638
Woodstock, GA 30188-1383

Toll Free: 1 (888) 264-5877
Phone: (770) 928-2834
Fax: 1 (866) 827-3240
Web site: www.americanbookcompany.com

About the Authors:

Sara Hinton has a B.A. from Columbia University and an M.A. in The Teaching of English from Teachers College, Columbia University. She taught middle school language arts and college courses in writing, grammar, and literature for several years.

Kristie Smith is a language arts teacher in the Georgia Public School System. Since 2000, she has taught a variety of language arts and English courses ranging from the middle grades through the college level. Her Ed.S. degree is from Mercer University.

Leah Ott has a B.A. from Evangel University and an M.Ed. in English Education from the University of Georgia. She has taught Language Arts in high school for several years and currently teaches Gifted Language Arts at the middle school level.

Lisa M. Cocca is a former elementary and middle school teacher and librarian. She writes language arts, social studies, and science materials for a wide range of ages.

About the Reviewer:

Karen H. Michael has been teaching for 17 years. Dr. Michael completed her doctorate at Purdue University in 2002 in literacy and language education. Since 2000, she is an assistant professor in the Tift College of Education at Mercer University. She has four publications and has made more than 25 presentations at local, regional, and international conferences. Dr. Michael has trained many elementary and middle school language arts/reading teachers in Georgia, South Carolina, and Indiana through professional development courses.

About the Project Coordinator:

Zuzana Urbanek serves as ELA Curriculum Coordinator for American Book Company. She is a professional writer with 25 years of experience in education, business, and publishing. She has taught a variety of English courses since 1990 at the college level and also taught English as a foreign language abroad. Her master's degree is from Arizona State University.

About the Executive Editor:

Dr. Frank J. Pintozzi is a former Professor of Education at Kennesaw State University. For over 28 years, he has taught English and reading at the high school and college levels as well as in teacher preparation courses in language arts and social studies. In addition to writing and editing state standard-specific texts for high school exit and end of course exams, he has edited and written numerous college textbooks.

Test Taking Tips

1. Complete the chapters and practice tests in this book.

2. Before the test, enjoy a good night's sleep and a good breakfast. Find your classroom and get settled.

3. Think success. Keep your thoughts positive. Tell yourself you will do well on the test.

4. Read directions carefully. If you don't understand them, ask for further explanation.

5. Some people like to skim questions and answers before reading a passage. Others prefer to read the passage before looking at the answers. Decide which approach works best for you.

6. If you are not sure of an answer, take an educated guess. Eliminate choices that are definitely wrong, and then choose from the remaining answers.

7. Use your answer sheet correctly. Make sure the number on your question matches the number on your answer sheet. If you need to change an answer, erase it completely.

8. Check your answers. Review your exam to make sure you have chosen the best responses. Change answers only if you are sure they are wrong.

Mastering the Georgia 4th Grade CRCT in Reading

Diagnostic Test

The purpose of this diagnostic test is to measure your knowledge in reading comprehension. This diagnostic test is based on the Georgia Performance Standards for Reading and adheres to the sample question format provided by the Georgia Department of Education.

General Directions:

1. Read all directions carefully.

2. Read each question or sample. Then choose the best answer.

3. Choose only one answer for each question. If you change an answer, be sure to erase your original answer completely.

4. After taking the test, you or your instructor should score it using the evaluation chart following the test. This will enable you to determine your strengths and weaknesses.

Section 1

Kumi and the Tako

Kumi gazed up into the cloudless sky. Next week, her whole family would gather here for the kite festival. The sky would be a patchwork quilt of kites. Her family had made a tako, or kite, for the festival too. Kumi had helped her grandfather paint the dancing doll onto the delicate rice paper. People of all ages would bring their homemade bamboo and rice paper takos to the festival. Hand painted fish, turtles, birds, and dragons would join the paper dolls in flight. Kite runners would stand shoulder to shoulder pulling on cords controlling their takos. Kumi's brother would have the honor of flying their family's kite.

Kumi could feel the excitement building inside of her. A week was so long to wait! Then, she spotted a young man down by the water. He was holding some cord and folding and unfolding his body. At last he began running while tugging at the cord. Finally, the wind caught hold of the tako. Up, up it went. Diamond after diamond it raised into the sky. It was a kite train with more than one hundred colorful diamonds all attached to a single cord! The young man struggled to keep control of his creation. The kite train swooped and dipped and turned. It looked like a rainbow dancing in the sky. Kumi watched the kite train for nearly an hour. Then, the young man, exhausted by his battle with nature, cut the cord and watched his kite train sail away.

1. Which of the following words means the same as *exhausted*? 4R1i Lit

   A. angry

   B. weary

   C. relaxed

   D. amused

2. Which sentence contains a metaphor? 4R1d Lit

   A. Kumi gazed up into the cloudless sky.

   B. The sky would be a patchwork quilt of kites.

   C. Finally, the wind caught hold of the tako.

   D. It looked like a rainbow dancing in the sky.

3. Why does the young man cut the kite cord? 4R1b Lit

   A. He is tired from flying his kite.

   B. He wants a different kite to fly.

   C. Kumi asks him to release the kite.

   D. The kite is easier to control with a shorter cord.

4. Who is telling the story? 4R1c Lit

   A. Kumi

   B. a narrator

   C. Kumi's brother

   D. the young man

5. How does Kumi MOST LIKELY feel about her family kite? 4R1f Lit

   A. She wishes they had made a kite train instead.

   B. She feels jealous because her brother was flying it.

   C. She feels proud of the work she and her grandfather did.

   D. She is disappointed because she wanted to paint a bird on it.

Pet Pigs

Potbellied pigs are becoming popular pets. The number of people buying pet pigs is growing. Unfortunately, the number of pigs left in shelters is growing too. It is important to think about both the pros and cons of pig ownership.

Pigs are very smart animals. It is fairly easy to train them. Pigs can use a litter box or a certain corner of a yard as a bathroom. They can learn many different tricks and respond to many commands. However, because pigs are so smart, they can get bored easily. A pig kept in the house all day will look for ways to entertain himself. Chewing up rugs is one way pigs stay busy inside. Knocking over house plants and digging through the dirt is another way that pigs have fun.

Pigs are also very social animals. They are friendly and playful. Many people find their sweet nature charming. However, those same traits are also a reason people give up their pigs. Many people can't handle the amount of attention their pig demands. Also, pigs are herd animals. When you adopt a pig into your family, the pig sees your family as members of its herd. When the pig is about eighteen months old, it tries to become the "top pig." It will fight for the number one spot in the pecking order of the herd. The pig will charge at or snap at the people in the house. This can get dangerous.

Most pigs enjoy good health. With proper care, they can live ten to fifteen years. Owners should bring their pigs to a veterinarian for a checkup once a year. The vet will give the pigs the vaccinations they need to stay healthy. The vet will also trim the pig's hooves every year. Even with good care, one of the biggest threats to a pig's health is pneumonia. Weather plays a big part in this, but so does stress. Pigs are very sensitive animals. They can easily have their feelings hurt or become "stressed out" by family activities. Pigs have small lungs. Stress makes it harder for the pigs to fight off germs that affect the lungs.

Potbellied pigs make fun pets. They also require a great amount of care. Think carefully about the time and work involved before you make a pig your pet.

6. What is the main idea of   4R1f Inf
   this passage?

   A. Pigs can't handle the stress of living with people.

   B. Pigs want to be the ones in charge of the family.

   C. People like pigs because they are smarter than cats and dogs.

   D. People should think carefully before getting a pig as a pet.

7. Why would a pet pig   4R1e Inf
   chew up a rug?

   A. It is bored.

   B. It is angry.

   C. It is hungry.

   D. It is scared.

8. What is a reason people   4R1a Inf
   give up their pet pigs?

   A. Pigs are easy to train.

   B. Pigs have a sweet nature.

   C. Pigs need lots of attention.

   D. Pigs are not healthy animals.

9. Which sentence from   4R1h Inf
   the passage is an
   opinion?

   A. The number of people buying pet pigs is growing.

   B. Chewing up rugs is one way pigs stay busy inside.

   C. Also, pigs are herd animals.

   D. Potbellied pigs make fun pets.

10. The word *fortunately*   4R3e
    means "in a lucky way."
    The word *unfortunately* means

    A. "in a very lucky way."

    B. "not in a lucky way."

    C. "in a nearly lucky way."

    D. "in a much too lucky way."

O Say Can You See

The year was 1814, when Francis Scott Key

Penned those special words, "O say can you see."

He paid honor to three colors: red, white, and blue,

And to the men in the harbor where Old Glory flew.   [line 4]

In schools and in ballparks, his words still ring out,

Reminding us of those who fought without a doubt.

Such dangers they faced protecting the land they knew,

Such dangers that would meet their followers too.   [line 8]

His words still remind every girl and every boy

Of the freedoms that we still gratefully enjoy,

And of the heroes of yesterday and today,

Who have made freedom the American way.   [line 12]

11. Which pair of words found in the poem rhyme? `4R1i Lit`

A. see, blue

B. out, doubt

C. boy, way

D. enjoy, today

12. As it is used in the poem, the word *ring* means `4R3h`

A. to circle around.

B. to call with a bell.

C. to make a telephone call.

D. to announce many times.

13. How does the author show it is difficult to defend freedom? `4R1i Lit`

A. by repeating the *s* sound in line 1

B. by including the year 1814 in line 1

C. by using end rhyme throughout the poem

D. by repeating the word *dangers* in lines 7 and 8

14. According to the poem, how are yesterday's and today's heroes alike? `4R1g Lit`

A. All heroes are men.

B. All heroes like sports.

C. All have helped us live freely.

D. All have fought in ship harbors.

15. What point of view is used in this poem? `4R1c Lit`

A. first person

B. second person

C. third person

D. fourth person

What's Cooking?

Cooking schools give lessons to people young and old. It seems like everyone wants to learn how to cook and bake. Cooking schools exist to make sure the future chefs learn how to do it right.

One of the first things students learn is how to safely prepare food. They learn how to clean fruits and vegetables and how to handle raw foods. They learn which foods must be kept separate from other foods. Safety lessons don't stop with food handling. Students need common sense in the kitchen. They need to know how to handle sharp knives and to work carefully around a hot stove.

Then, the fun begins. Students learn how to prepare family favorites and a few foods they have never tasted before. In some classes, they learn to make tasty, healthy snacks. In other classes, students prepare whole meals. Some of the most popular classes in cooking schools are the baking classes. Some students have to wait a full year to get into a baking class. The future pastry chefs practice mixing, kneading, and rolling the sweet batters and doughs. The classrooms fill with the scents of cookies, cakes, pies, and breads baking. Then, the best part of the class begins. The chefs eat their delicious accomplishments.

You can find cooking classes in almost every area in the country. Check your newspapers or phone book to find a class near your home. Before long, you will become the family chef.

16. What is the topic sentence in paragraph 2? 4R1b Inf

   A. One of the first things students learn is how to safely prepare food.

   B. They learn how to clean fruits and vegetables and how to handle raw foods.

   C. They need to know how to handle sharp knives and to work carefully around a hot stove.

   D. Students learn how to prepare family favorites and a few foods they have never tasted before.

17. Which sentence is an opinion? 4R1h Inf

   A. Cooking schools exist to make sure the future chefs learn how to do it right.

   B. Then, the best part of the class begins.

   C. In other classes, students prepare whole meals.

   D. You can find cooking classes in almost every area in the country.

18. What is one of the first things students learn in cooking school? 4R1a Inf

   A. how to make healthy snacks

   B. where to find classes near home

   C. how to mix and knead dough

   D. how to clean fruits and vegetables

19. Which is the best summary of the passage? 4R1f Inf

   A. The student chefs can eat everything they bake.

   B. There are cooking schools all around the country.

   C. Cooking schools teach people how to safely make healthy, tasty food.

   D. Everyone in cooking school wants to learn how to bake sweet foods.

20. What two words from the passage are homophones? 4R3b

   A. scents and sense

   B. cook and bake

   C. family and favorites

   D. batters and doughs

The Case of the Uninvited Visitor

Jake shut his bedroom door. He didn't want Buster drooling all over the evidence. Buster was a great dog, but Jake didn't have time to waste on wiping up dog spit. Jake knew that, to solve this mystery, he would have to concentrate.

He dumped the contents of his shoe box on the floor. Then, he opened his notebook and read the first entry: "broken harmonica, left corner of backyard, Monday." Jake looked closely at the harmonica. Why did it look familiar? He grabbed his magnifying glass and examined it again. This time he noticed the initials, RR, scratched into the metal. Jake said, "This belongs to Rick Roberts. I'm sure I've identified the harmonica's owner correctly." Jake wrote "SUSPECTS" in his notebook. Under it, he wrote, "Rick Roberts."

Next, Jake picked up the orange-striped scarf. After studying it he said, "This belongs to Mr. White. Why would he come into our yard?" Jake added Mr. White's name to his suspect list.

Then, Jake picked up the pink garden glove. He closed his eyes and attempted to picture someone wearing the glove. Finally, he remembered where he had seen it. Mrs. Malloy was working in her garden yesterday. Her right hand was bare; however, her left hand was wearing a pink garden glove. Jake added Mrs. Malloy's name to his suspect list.

Jake heard Buster barking. Looking out his bedroom window, Jake saw Buster in the left back corner of the yard. None of his suspects were in sight. Jake shook his head. "I guess you're trying to protect us, but I wish you had barked when our uninvited guest appeared in our yard."

Jake reviewed the information in his notebook. Each item had been found in the same corner of the yard. Each item had appeared on a different day and belonged to a different neighbor. Jake returned to the window. Buster had quieted, so Jake wanted to be certain his pet was not getting into mischief. Jake remembered his mother's reaction the last time Buster pulled the clean laundry off the clothesline.

Jake didn't see Buster in the yard. Had one of his neighbors kidnapped Buster? He raced outside and spotted Buster crawling under the fence. When Jake reached Buster, his dog dropped a stuffed toy bunny on the ground and wagged his tail. "Oh, Buster," Jake moaned, "you are the uninvited visitor."

21. In paragraph 5, why does the author tell us where Buster is in the yard?

A. to show why Jake can concentrate on the case

B. to hint that Buster may be the uninvited guest

C. to explain why Jake's neighbors were not there

D. to paint a picture of the yard in readers' minds

22. Based on the passage, what MOST LIKELY would Jake like to do?

A. knit a scarf

B. read a mystery

C. help with the laundry

D. visit with his neighbors

23. How were the three items Jake found alike?

A. They all belonged to the same neighbor.

B. They all were found on the same day.

C. They all were found in the same place.

D. They all were marked with the owner's initials.

24. What did Jake do to help him remember who owned the glove?

A. He looked for Mrs. Malloy's initials on the gloves.

B. He looked closely at the gloves with a magnifying glass.

C. He went to Mrs. Malloy's house to see if she was wearing gloves.

D. He closed his eyes and tried to picture someone wearing the glove.

25. Use the dictionary entry to answer the question.

> **examine** (n.) (1) to look at closely; (2) to test the condition of; (3) to question carefully; (4) to test by questioning.

In Paragraph 2, what did Jake do when he examined the harmonica?

A. He looked more closely at the harmonica.

B. He checked to see if the harmonica worked.

C. He asked Buster if he had seen anyone with a harmonica.

D. He wrote down a list of questions he wanted Rick to answer.

Section 2

John Philip Sousa

John Philip Sousa had a special way of composing music. Most composers work with a piano so they can hear the notes as they write them. Sousa didn't need a piano. He could hear the music playing in his head. His "brain-band" meant he could write his music anywhere. If he was inspired to do so, he could compose music on a train or a ship, or in a park or a hotel.

Sousa believed the key to writing great music was to write when he felt inspired. Only then could he write music that would inspire others. Sousa was moved to compose by all kinds of things. Sousa had a great love for his country. The United States was one of his greatest inspirations. Sousa wrote many marches that moved other people to share in that love.

Sousa let his imagination run wild while he was writing music. He would picture the scenes he wanted to express in his music. Then, his "brain-band" would take over. Sousa listened to the music playing in his head. He had a gift for recognizing each note by name. Sometimes, it only took days for the whole song to come together in his mind. When the song was done, Sousa sat down with pen and paper and recorded what he had heard.

After Sousa wrote down the final note, he would turn the last page of the music on its side. Then, he would sign his name and the date. Sousa would add one more piece of information to his signature. He would write down where he composed the music. Once the music was on paper, Sousa was ready to hear it played on the piano. Even though this was the first time he heard the music outside of his head, he rarely had to change a note.

Sousa's way of composing music was as successful as it was different. He wrote many marches in his lifetime. One of his best known marches is "Semper Fidelis." This song is now the official song of the US Marine Corps. Probably his most successful march is "Stars and Stripes Forever." It is the national march song of the United States. Bands still play that march in parades. In fact, Sousa was so successful at writing marches that he earned the nickname "The March King."

26. The passage is organized   4R1d Inf
in
A. time order.

B. process order.

C. cause and effect order.

D. question and answer order.

27. Another good title for   4R1f Inf
this passage is
A. "The March King and the Brain-Band"

B. "The Marine Corps Marching Song"

C. "The Music Makers"

D. "A Wild Imagination"

28. How did Sousa's signa-   4R1g Inf
ture help people know
more about how he worked?
A. It helped people see what moved him to write.

B. It proved he could write music very quickly.

C. It showed he wrote in many different places.

D. It told people he knew he would be famous.

29. How was Sousa differ-   4R1a Inf
ent from other
composers?
A. He wrote marches for bands.

B. He lived in the United States.

C. He wrote music without a piano.

D. He knew the names of the notes.

30. The word *imagination*   4R3c
comes from the root word
imag, meaning "likeness." What
does the word *imagination*
mean?
A. ability to hear music naturally

B. ability to make friends easily

C. ability to write notes from memory

D. ability to picture things with the mind

The Brothers' Journey

Long ago, two brothers were invited to a feast in a faraway palace. After beginning their journey, they noticed a man standing beside a cart with a broken wheel. The first brother said to the second, "Let's stop and help."

The second brother said, "We will be late for the feast if we stop."

The two brothers could not agree. So the second brother continued walking, while the first brother stopped. When the wheel was repaired, the man offered him a ride in his cart.

So the first brother rode along until he reached his brother. Then, he thanked the man and continued his journey on foot.

Further along their journey, the brothers saw a woman struggling with a wagon filled with apples. The first brother said to the second, "Let's stop and help."

The second brother said, "We will be late for the feast if we stop."

The two brothers could not agree. So the second brother continued walking, while the first brother stopped. After the brother pulled the wagon to the marketplace, the woman wrapped six apples in a cloth for him. He thanked her and hurried along his way.

When the brothers were together again, the first brother offered his brother some apples. "No," the second brother answered. "They might ruin my appetite for the fine foods at the feast."

So the first brother ate two apples and saved the others. Soon the brothers spotted a man and a donkey. The man could not make the stubborn donkey move. The first brother said to the second, "Let's stop and help."

The second brother said, "We will be late for the feast if we stop."

The two brothers could not agree. So the second brother continued walking, while the first brother stopped. Being as clever as he was kind, he held an apple in front of the donkey, and soon the donkey was walking. He gave the man the remaining apples. To show his gratitude, the man handed the brother shoes and said, "These are the finest shoes I've ever made. You will be walking on clouds in these."

The first brother thanked the man and hurried to meet his brother. Finally, the brothers reached the palace and were told the feast was the following week. The second brother felt angry, having wasted his morning on the journey. The first brother felt happy, grateful for the gifts he had received.

31. The way the characters   4R1b Lit
travel from place to
place helps readers know more
about
   A. who else will be going to the
feast.

   B. the time in which the story
takes place.

   C. why the brothers are such
good friends.

   D. why the brothers were invited
to the feast.

32. Who is telling the story?   4R1c Lit
   A. the narrator

   B. the first brother

   C. the second brother

   D. the man with the donkey

33. What does, "You will   4R1d Lit
be walking on clouds in
these" mean?
   A. The shoes can help people fly.

   B. The shoes are very
comfortable.

   C. The shoes are blue and white.

   D. The shoes won't get wet in the
rain.

34. What is the theme of this   4R1h Lit
tale?
   A. It is important to be on time.

   B. A stubborn animal can be
tamed.

   C. Helping people is worth the
time.

   D. Brothers share both the work
and the rewards.

35. As it is used in this story,   4R3a
the word *gratitude* means
   A. "the act of bragging."

   B. "a useful skill or craft."

   C. "learning from another
person."

   D. "being thankful for a
kindness."

36. What will the second   4R1f Lit
brother MOST likely do
if he meets someone in need on
the way home?
   A. stop and help

   B. keep walking home

   C. tell his brother to help

   D. invite the person to the feast

Peaches and Nectarines

If you asked most people how peaches and nectarines are different, their answer would be, "fuzz." A peach has a fuzzy skin, while a nectarine has a smooth skin. The fuzz may be the first thing you notice, but it isn't the only difference. It's true both fruits have a yellow or white flesh. They even both belong to the same fruit family. However, nectarines tend to be smaller than peaches. They also often have more red on the skin. If you cut into both fruits, you will notice a stronger scent coming from the nectarine. Both fruits taste sweet and juicy. However, the nectarine has twice as much vitamin A as the peach. It also has more vitamin C and potassium. Still, the peach is the queen of fruits in the United States. The only fruit more popular is the apple.

	Peaches	Nectarines
Touch	fuzzy	smooth
Look	red blush to the skin; yellow or white flesh	more red in the skin than peaches; yellow or white flesh
Smell	sweet	sweet and strong
Taste	sweet and juicy	sweet and juicy
Health	vitamin A; vitamin C; potassium	2X vitamin A of peaches; more vitamin C; more potassium

37. According to the chart, 4R1c Inf
compared to peaches,
nectarines have twice as much

A. juice.

B. scent.

C. vitamin A.

D. potassium.

38. Most people think the 4R1a Inf
difference between a
peach and a nectarine is the way
the fruits

A. feel.

B. look.

C. smell.

D. taste.

39. Which is the topic sen- 4R1b Inf
tence in this passage?

A. If you asked most people how
peaches and nectarines are
different, their answer would
be, "fuzz."

B. A peach has a fuzzy skin,
while a nectarine has a
smooth skin.

C. The fuzz may be the first
thing you notice, but it isn't
the only difference.

D. Still, the peach is the queen of
fruits in the United States.

40. The word *popular* comes 4R3c
from the root word *pop,*
meaning "people." What does
the word *popular* mean?

A. liked by many

B. good for health

C. sweet and juicy

D. grown on trees

41. The antonym of *sweet* is 4R3i

A. *hard.*

B. *sour.*

C. *tasty.*

D. *darling.*

Success!

I blinked several times—a Crazy 4 Coconut Bar! "Mom," I whispered, pointing at the prize.

"No, David," she said. "You didn't eat the last three candy bars I purchased."

Poor Mom, she didn't understand. The thrill wasn't in eating the candy; it was in discovering the treasure. Last winter, I had found a list on the Internet of the most difficult candies to find. My goal was to locate each of them, and that coconut bar was the final undiscovered item in my chocolate bar column. True, I won't eat the candy, but I need that wrapper for my collection. I can't come this close to victory and let it slip through my fingers. "Mom," I begged.

"It's a waste of money," she answered.

A waste of money! How could anyone describe the feeling of success as a waste of money? I needed a foolproof plan, and I needed it immediately. "What if I buy it with my own money?" I asked.

"You'll spend your own money on a candy bar you won't even eat?"

"It's for Matt. He loves coconut, and he has been really sad since his lizard disappeared." This is true; plus, Matt won't care about my keeping the wrapper.

Finally, Mom said, "Okay."

I cradled the coconut candy in my hands and thought about what I had achieved. I had located each item in the column and had the wrappers as proof. Today, I tasted victory; tomorrow, I will start on the fruity candy column.

42. Why did David want the 4R1b Lit
    candy bar?

    A. He loves candy.

    B. He wanted the wrapper.

    C. He wanted to give it to his
       friend.

    D. He didn't like the other candy
       he had.

43. Who is telling the story? 4R1c Lit

    A. Mom

    B. Matt

    C. David

    D. the narrator

44. What word BEST 4R1f Lit
    describes David?

    A. gloomy

    B. starving

    C. insecure

    D. focused

45. Which phrase is an 4R1d Lit
    example of alliteration?

    A. a foolproof plan

    B. a waste of money

    C. slip through my fingers

    D. cradled the coconut candy

46. Where did David find 4R1b Lit
    the candy list?

    A. on the Internet

    B. Matt gave it to him

    C. in the candy store

    D. on a treasure hunt

InfoWeb.net

Abraham Lincoln [Search]

Family

Jobs

Presidency

Speeches

Photos

Quizzes and
Fun Activities

Abraham Lincoln

Sixteenth President

Born: February 12, 1809
Died: April 15, 1869

Abraham Lincoln loved to
read and walk in nature. He
never went to college, but he became President of
the United States. His favorite foods were fruit salad
and cheese and crackers. Lincoln was the tallest
president. He stood 6 feet and 4 inches tall. His
image is on the front of the Lincoln penny.

47. This information is an   4LSV2a
    example of a

    A. Web page.

    B. textbook.

    C. magazine ad.

    D. TV program.

48. If you wanted to play a   4LSV2c
    game about the presi-
    dent's pets, you would click on

    A. Family.

    B. Photos.

    C. Presidency.

    D. Quizzes and Fun Activities.

49. The author probably   4LSV2b
    wrote this information
    to

    A. inform readers about
       Lincoln's life and work.

    B. convince readers Lincoln was
       the best president.

    C. sell readers a book about Lin-
       coln.

    D. tell readers an interesting
       story.

50. In the passage, the word   4R3c
    nature means

    A. "tone."

    B. "gift."

    C. "outdoors."

    D. "character."

EVALUATION CHART FOR GEORGIA 4TH GRADE CRCT IN READING DIAGNOSTIC TEST

Directions: On the following chart, circle the question numbers that you answered incorrectly and evaluate the results. Then turn to the appropriate chapters, read the explanations, and complete the exercises. Review other chapters as needed. Finally, complete the post-test(s) to assess your progress and further prepare you for the **Georgia 4th Grade Reading CRCT.**

*Note: Some question numbers will appear under multiple chapters because those questions require demonstration of multiple skills.

Chapters	Diagnostic Test Question
Chapter 1: Word Parts	10, 30, 40, 50
Chapter 2: Learning New Words	20, 25, 35
Chapter 3: Word Meanings	12, 41
Chapter 4: Reading for Information	8, 9, 17, 18, 29, 38
Chapter 5: How Information is Organized	7, 16, 26, 39
Chapter 6: Predictions and Conclusions	28
Chapter 7: Graphics	37
Chapter 8: Reading Literature	3, 4, 5, 15, 21, 22, 24, 31, 32, 36, 42, 43, 44, 46
Chapter 9: Literary Devices	2, 33, 45
Chapter 10: Themes and Lessons in Literature	34
Chapter 11: Literature and an Author's Life	14, 23
Chapter 12: Media in Our Lives	47, 48, 49

Chapter 1
Word Parts

This chapter addresses the following GPS-based CRCT standard(s):

> **ELA4R3** The student understands and acquires new vocabulary and uses it correctly in reading and writing. The student
> **c.** Identifies the meaning of common root words to determine the meaning of unfamiliar words.
> **e.** Identifies the meaning of common prefixes (e.g., un-, re-, dis-).

Everyone has come across unknown words while reading. Some people have a way to figure out what those unknown words mean without knowing the full dictionary definition. The secret is to know what the parts of words mean. If you can get to know the common parts of words, then it will make things easier for you when you do come across one of those new words. It is like knowing parts of a puzzle. If you know what some of the parts mean, you can figure out the meaning of the word with more success.

ROOT WORDS

What is a **root word**? A root word is the smallest part of a word. Prefixes and suffixes are built on that small part. It's like a house being build on a frame. Root words are in common words that you use like *autograph, credit, judge, male, succeed,* and *phone.* The chart on the

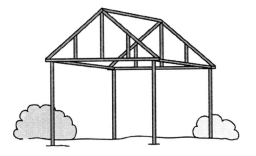

next page lists some of the most common roots words and their meanings.

Common Root Words

Root	Definition	Example
bio	life	biodome
cede, ceed, cess	go, yield	recede, process
chron	time	synchronize
cred	believe	incredible
dict	speak	dictate
equ	equal	equate
geo, terr, terra	earth	geography, terrestrial
graph	writing	telegraph
ject	throw	project
jud, jur, jus	law, justice	jury
metri, meter	measure	perimeter
naut, naus, nav	sea, ships, or travelers	navigate
ped, pod	foot	pedestrian
phon, phono, phone	sound	microphone
rupt	break	interrupt
scrib, script	write	scribble
temp	time, season	tempest
vers, vert	turn	convert

Practice 1: Root Words

ELA4R3c

Read each question, and pick the answer that best answers the question.

1. Which of these is the root word of the word *antibiotics* in the sentence?

   > Jack gave the dog <u>antibiotics</u> for the bad scratch on its paw.

   A. anti   B. tics   C. tibi   D. bio

2. Which definition BEST represents the meaning of *reject* in the sentence?

   > We decided to <u>reject</u> the most expensive vacation option this year.

   A. accept for the first time   C. not accept

   B. accept again   D. consider

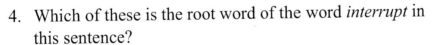

3. Which definition BEST represents the meaning of *photograph* in the sentence?

   > Benjie liked to take <u>photographs</u> of his friends and family on special occasions.

   A. pictures   C. paintings

   B. drawings   D. films

4. Which of these is the root word of the word *interrupt* in this sentence?

   > Mother said not to <u>interrupt</u> her nap unless it was an emergency.

   A. in   B. ter   C. rupt   D. interr

5. Which of these is the root word of the word *naval* in the sentence?

   > We are so proud of our son who just left for the <u>naval</u> academy.

   A. na   B. nav   C. val   D. al

6. Which of these is the root word of the word *autograph* in the sentence?

   I got the <u>autographs</u> of the Jonas Brothers at the concert last night.

   A. graph

   B. auto

   C. togr

   D. raph

7. Based on the root, what is the definition of the word *tripod* in the sentence?

   We put the camera on the <u>tripod</u> before taking the family photo.

   A. falling down

   B. lever for pushing

   C. three-footed stand

   D. long pole

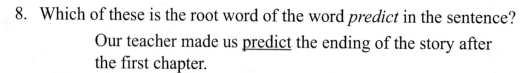

8. Which of these is the root word of the word *predict* in the sentence?

   Our teacher made us <u>predict</u> the ending of the story after the first chapter.

   A. pre

   B. pred

   C. dict

   D. edict

PREFIXES

What is a **prefix**? A prefix is a small part that is added onto the root word to change the meaning or add to the meaning of the root word. Root words can often become prefixes. A prefix always comes at the beginning of a word. In the chart below, you will find a list of common prefixes and their meanings.

<table>
<tr><th colspan="3">Common Prefixes</th></tr>
<tr><th>Prefix</th><th>Definition</th><th>Example</th></tr>
<tr><td>auto</td><td>self</td><td>autograph</td></tr>
<tr><td>anti</td><td>against</td><td>antibody</td></tr>
<tr><td>bi</td><td>two</td><td>binoculars</td></tr>
<tr><td>co, con, com</td><td>with</td><td>compare</td></tr>
<tr><td>de</td><td>from, away, down</td><td>depart</td></tr>
<tr><td>dis, diff</td><td>apart, not, negative</td><td>disarm</td></tr>
<tr><td>ex</td><td>out, away from</td><td>expel</td></tr>
<tr><td>il, un, ir, im, in</td><td>not</td><td>illogical, impatient</td></tr>
<tr><td>mis</td><td>without, bad, badly</td><td>mistrust</td></tr>
<tr><td>multi</td><td>many</td><td>multiple</td></tr>
<tr><td>per</td><td>through</td><td>permeate</td></tr>
<tr><td>pre</td><td>before</td><td>preface</td></tr>
<tr><td>pro</td><td>forward</td><td>proceed</td></tr>
<tr><td>re</td><td>again</td><td>reread</td></tr>
<tr><td>tele</td><td>distant, far off</td><td>telescope</td></tr>
<tr><td>trans</td><td>across</td><td>transport</td></tr>
<tr><td>tri</td><td>three</td><td>triangle</td></tr>
<tr><td>uni</td><td>one</td><td>uniform</td></tr>
</table>

Practice 2: Prefixes
ELA4R3e

1. Which prefix creates the right meaning for the word in the sentence?

    We rode our ___cycles on the beach. (two wheels)

    A. mid   B. bi   C. pre   D. tele

2. Which prefix creates the right meaning for the word in the sentence?

    Benjamin Franklin wrote his _____biography. (self)

    A. re   C. sub

    B. multi   D. auto

Benjamin Franklin

3. Which prefix creates the right meaning for the word in the sentence?

    We had to _____mit our location over the radio. (across)

    A. trans   C. anti

    B. geo   D. com

4. Which prefix creates the right meaning for the word in the sentence?

    You do not rob a bank because it is _____legal and wrong. (not)

    A. dis   C. anti

    B. con   D. il

5. Which prefix creates the right meaning for the word in the sentence?

> We had to ___test the students. (again)

A. post   C. pre

B. re   D. auto

6. Which prefix creates the right meaning for the word in the sentence?

> My dad got a ___motion to a better job. (forward)

A. per   C. re

B. pro   D. pre

ACTIVITY: MAKING NEW WORDS

Using the roots and prefixes below, see how many words you can make. You can add more than just one prefix and root together. Share your list with a classmate and your teacher.

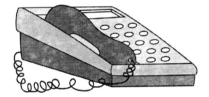

Examples:

- prefix *tele* plus root *phone* makes *telephone*
- prefix *ex* plus root *vert* (plus *tro*) makes *extrovert*

Root Words		Prefixes	
bio	naut, naus, nav	anti	pro
chron	ped, pod	auto	re
cred	phon, phono, phone	co, con, com	tele
dict	scrib, script	ex	trans
equ	temp, time	multi	tri
graph	vers, vert	pre	uni

SUFFIXES

What is a **suffix**, and how is it used? A suffix is added at the end of a word to add to the meaning or to make a new word. A word can have more than one suffix at the end. For example, one can be joy*ful*, joy*less*, joy*ous*. Or a person is a work*er* or work*less*, and a problem can be work*able*. The following table lists some common suffixes and their meanings.

Common Suffixes		
Suffix	**Definition**	**Example**
able, ible	can be done	workable
al, ial	have characteristic of	amiable
er, or	one who takes part in	farmer
ful	full of	joyful
ion	act or process	violation
ist	one who is or practices	violinist
less	without	motionless
ly	characteristic of	friendly
ment	process, action	involvement
ness	quality of being	happiness
ology	study of	biology
ous	possessing the quality of	wondrous
y	characterized by	wordy

Practice 3: Suffixes

1. Which suffix completes the sentence below?

    We will be paid upon complet_____ of the job.

    A. ness   B. able   C. ion   D. ment

2. In the sentence below, which word has a suffix added to it?

    Robbie was irritable because he did not have a nap.

    A. because   B. irritable   C. have   D. Robbie

3. Which suffixes complete the sentence below?

    Our vaca____ was very rest____.

    A. ment, less   C. tion, able

    B. ful, tion   D. tion, ful

4. Which suffixes complete the sentence below?

    Isabella accepted the birthday gift
    cheer___ ___.

    A. ful, ly   C. ment, ly

    B. ous, y   D. less, y

COMBINING PARTS OF WORDS

Words parts are root words, prefixes, and suffixes. We **combine word parts** to form words. For example, if you know that *re* means "again" and *viv* means "life," you can put them together to form the word *revive*. Then, you can figure out that *revive* means "to come to life or live again." With that information, you can look at your choices on the test and find the definition that most closely matches this meaning. Knowing the meanings of word parts does not mean that a definition will match perfectly. You have to judge which definition is best for what you know about the parts of a word.

Example:

- *Auto* (self) + *bio* (life) + *graph* (write) + *y* (characterized by) = a person's own written account of his or her life

Practice 4: Combining Word Parts
ELA4R3c, e

1. Choose the definition that BEST fits the word combination below.

geo + graphy = geography

A. study of the earth's surface

B. characterized by earth

C. cave writings

D. writing in the dirt

2. Choose the definition that BEST fits the word combination below.

un + fortunate = unfortunate

A. very wealthy

B. very lucky

C. missed by luck

D. thrifty

3. Choose the definition that BEST fits the word combination below.

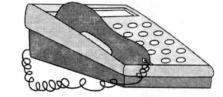

tele + phone = telephone

A. device to carry sound over a long distance

B. device to break sound up

C. device to interrupt sound

D. device to write message over a long distance

4. From the sentence below, choose the definition that BEST matches the meaning of the word *manually* as it is used in the sentence.

The pilot had to fly the plane <u>manually</u>.

A. with a computer

B. using a hand crank

C. with another person

D. using a hand-held controller

5. From the sentence below, choose the definition that BEST matches the meaning of the word *disrupted* as it is used in the sentence.

The barking dog <u>disrupted</u> my sleep.

A. broke up the silence and order of

B. separated the truth

C. made louder

D. broke the window apart

Chapter 1 Summary

Knowing word parts is a skill that will make you a better reader and help you succeed on tests! When you encounter words that you do not know, look at individual parts to figure out what the word means without looking in the dictionary.

Root words are the smallest parts of a word.

Prefixes and **suffixes** hook onto root words to form new words. They are like parts of a puzzle. The individual parts are put together to form the big picture…or the bigger word!

Chapter 1 Review

ELA4R3c, e

Read the paragraph, and answer the questions that follow.

The great white shark is a big fish. The movie *Jaws* made many people afraid of sharks. Great whites are actually protected in the United States. This means that people cannot fish for great whites. In the past, the great White has been <u>overfished</u>, which is ___fortunate. Marine <u>biologists</u> have found these sharks to be social animals. One place that marine biologists watch great whites is in False Bay, South Africa. The sharks hunt seals by attacking from <u>beneath</u> the seal. Also, it has been <u>discovered</u> that the sharks are very intelligent and curious. They have a very good sense of smell. Great whites can smell blood from over a mile away. Scientists still do not know very much about great whites.

1. The prefix *over* before *fished* means that

    A. no one wanted to fish for sharks.

    B. people only caught sharks from above.

    C. fishers caught too many sharks.

    D. fishers caught too few sharks.

2. Which prefix means "not" and can be added to the word *fortunate* in the sentence?

    > In the past, the great white has been <u>overfished</u>, which is ___fortunate.

    A. mis   B. anti   C. con   D. un

3. Which definition BEST fits the meaning of the word *biologist* as it is used in the paragraph?

    A. study of water

    B. person who kills fish

    C. one who studies living organisms

    D. someone who catches fish for food

4. In the word *beneath, be* means

    A. characterized by

    B. cause to be

    C. in place of

    D. distant from

5. In the word *discovered, dis* means

    A. badly   B. speak   C. not   D. with

Read the story, and answer the questions that follow.

> Mrs. Cunningham stood in front of the class. Her face was sad. She said, "I can't believe how poorly everyone did on their paragraphs." She looked slowly at each student's face. Then, she began passing out our paragraphs. I had not tried very hard on the assignment. My paragraph had red all over it. The grade was a D-. Tears gathered in my eyes. I had never made such a bad grade before. After she passed out the papers, she went to the front again. She said, "Everyone is going to rewrite these paragraphs until we succeed!" We began writing. The sun shone in the windows making the class temperature rise. Mrs. Cunningham turned on fans to make it more comfortable. We worked all morning, rewriting our paragraphs to reverse the bad grades. By lunchtime, we all had succeeded in writing paragraphs worthy of A's. Mrs. Cunningham did a happy dance by her desk. We all laughed and clapped!

6. In the word *assignment*, what does the suffix *ment* mean?
   A. past action
   C. process or action

   B. characterized by
   D. quality of being

7. What does the root word *graph* mean in the word *paragraph*?
   A. hand   B. sound   C. listen   D. write

8. In the word *rewrite*, *re* means
   A. again   B. two   C. badly   D. hand

9. In the word *succeed*, *ceed* means
   A. believe   B. law   C. time   D. go

10. Which definition BEST fits the meaning of the word *reverse* in the paragraph?
   A. life back
   C. turn with in the same direction

   B. to move to the opposite
   D. to live again

Chapter 2
Learning New Words

This chapter addresses the following GPS-based CRCT standard(s):

ELA4R3 The student understands and acquires new vocabulary and uses it correctly in reading and writing. The student
a. Reads a variety of texts and incorporates new words into oral and written language
b. Determines the meaning of unknown words using their context
d. Determines meanings of words and alternate word choices using a dictionary and thesaurus

CONTEXT CLUES

Good readers use special skills to know what they read. Knowing how to use **context clues** is a good skill to have. A context clue is information around a word that helps you figure out its meaning. Be sure to use the clues in the sentence with the unknown word first. Then, look at the other sentences for help in understanding the unfamiliar word. Sometimes, nearby words have a similar meaning or give a definition.

Practice 1: Context Clues

ELA4R3a, b

Read the passage. Then, answer the questions that follow.

> Roaches have been around a long time. With over 5,000 <u>species</u> of roaches, they are not hard to find. Here are a few facts about cockroaches.
>
> • Some roaches can fly.
>
> • If ever stung by a stingray, you can mash up cockroaches to apply as a <u>poultice</u> to the wound.
>
> • A cockroach can live a week with no head. It dies from thirst.
>
> • A cockroach can carry many <u>disease</u>-producing organisms like bacteria.
>
> • Roaches use their <u>antennae</u> to smell.
>
> • Roaches have an <u>exoskeleton</u>. They shed their external skeletons several times a year.
>
> • Roaches can hold their breath for forty minutes at a time.
>
> • Roaches have no blood vessels. Blood just <u>slops</u> around inside them.

1. In this passage, the word *species* means
   A. "number."   B. "types."   C. "element."   D. "insects."

2. In this passage, the word *poultice* means
   A. "medicine paste."   C. "cloth."
   B. "bandage."   D. "bug."

3. What does the word *disease* mean as it is used in the passage?
   A. signs   B. energy   C. sickness   D. thirst

4. What does *antennae* mean?
   A. metal conductor on back

   B. sharp pointy teeth

   C. small nose

   D. movable organ on head

5. What does *exoskeleton* mean as it is used in the passage?
   A. a hard outer shell that protects the organs

   B. bones that support the inside of the insect

   C. a sticky substance the covers the legs

   D. hair covering the body of the insect

6. In the passage, *slops* means
   A. "flows in a circular pattern."

   B. "moves through tubes in body."

   C. "hardens in stomach."

   D. "moves wildly around in body."

USING A DICTIONARY

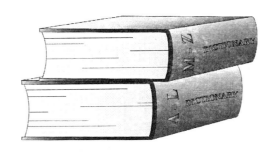

A **dictionary** is used to find the definitions of unfamiliar words. Did you know that a dictionary gives more than just a definition? It tells how to say a word. It also gives the part of speech. It is important to know how a dictionary is organized to make using it easy. Dictionaries are arranged in alphabetical order (ABC). On the top corner of each page, you will find two words called guide words. These words tell you the first word and the last word on that page. This helps you find the word you are looking for faster.

Practice 2: Using a Dictionary

ELA4R3d

Use the dictionary entry to answer the questions.

---

na·tion·al

[**nash**-*uh*-nl, **nash**-n*uh*]

adjective

   1 run by a federal government

   2 maintained by a nation as an independent political unit

   3 devoted to one's nation

noun

   4 a citizen of a nation or country

nat·u·ral

[**nach**-er-*uh*l, **nach**-r*uh*l]

adjective

   1 formed by nature

   2 uncultivated

   3 not treated, tanned, or spoiled by anything; in its original or
      raw state; *natural wood*

   4 in music neither flat nor sharp

noun

   5 a person who is successful at something without much
      practice or training

na·ture

[**ney**-cher]

noun

   1 the material world that exist outside human society

   2 the elements of the world: rivers, lakes, grass, animals

   3 the instincts that direct conduct

   4 a wild state or condition

idiom

   5 **by nature** inborn quality; *She is by nature a giving person.*

---

1. The *a* in the word *national* sounds MOST like the *a* in which word?

   A. apple   B. arm   C. saw   D. hate

2. Which sentence uses *nature* in the same way as definition number three?

   A. Anna likes to enjoy nature with long walks in the park.

   B. There are still undiscovered animals and plants in nature.

   C. The tigers in nature are just protecting themselves.

   D. It is her nature to be quiet and untalktive.

3. Which guide words would MOST likely mark this page?

   A. natatorial – natural

   B. nation – naught

   C. natheless – naturalist

   D. natron – naval

4. Which definition of the word *national* matches how it is used in the sentence below?

   The French national did not have to pay his parking ticket.

   A. 1   B. 2   C. 3   D. 4

5. Which sentence uses *natural* in the same way as definition number five?

   A. The fallen tree made a natural bridge across the creek.

   B. Jackson is a natural at playing the piano.

   C. The unplowed field was in a natural state.

   D. Elizabeth played a sharp note instead of a natural.

6. The *a* in the word *nature* sounds MOST like the *a* in which word below?

   A. talk   B. aid   C. father   D. hat

USING A THESAURUS

What is a **thesaurus**? It is a dictionary of
synonyms and antonyms. This means it
contains words that have the same meanings
or opposite meanings of the word that you are
looking for. It will also tell you words that

have meanings that are close to the same but not exactly the same. A thesaurus is
organized in alphabetical order (ABC) just like a dictionary. It is important to use
when you are writing. It can make a paragraph more interesting.

Practice 3:   Using a Thesaurus

ELA4R3d

Use the sample thesaurus to answer the questions.

---

peaceful
adjective
   1 synonym: calm, serene, placid, quiet; lack of emotion
related meanings: soft, gentle, mild, silent, noiseless
antonym: angry, turbulent
   2 synonym: stillness
related meanings: calm, hush, untroubled, tranquil

peak
noun
   1 synonym: mountain
related meanings: mount, alp, mesa, volcano
   2 synonym: summit
related meanings: pinnacle, climax, apex

---

1. Which word can replace *peaceful* in the sentence below?

    After her race, Jane looked <u>peaceful</u> but tired.

  A. angry   C. calm

  B. mild   D. silent

2. Which word for *peak* means the same as *summit*?
   A. apex
   B. mesa
   C. alp
   D. volcano

3. What part of speech are *calm* and *serene*?
   A. adjective   B. noun   C. adverb   D. verb

4. What guide words might mark the page that contains *peaceful* and *peak*?
   A. pass – pattern
   B. pathos – peace
   C. peculiar – pen
   D. paunch – peevish

5. Which word can replace the word *peaceful* in the sentence below?
   The water is <u>peaceful</u> today.
   A. hushed   B. turbulent   C. tranquil   D. lacking emotion

6. Which word means the opposite of *peaceful*?
   A. untroubled   B. calm   C. turbulent   D. still

CHAPTER 2 SUMMARY

A **context clue** is information around a new word that helps you figure out its meaning. First, use the clues in the sentence with the unknown word. Then, look at the other sentences in the passage for more help.

A **dictionary** has meanings of words. A dictionary also tells how to say a word and gives its part of speech. Dictionaries are arranged in alphabetical order (ABC).

A **thesaurus** is a dictionary of synonyms and antonyms. A thesaurus is organized in alphabetical order (ABC), just like a dictionary.

CHAPTER 2 REVIEW

ELA4R3a, b, d

Read the paragraph and answer the questions that follow.

> The air was full of excitement. Jack and Emily entered the theater with their parents. An <u>usher</u> helped them find their seats. The crowd quickly hummed with whispered conversation. Emily looked through her <u>program</u> to read about the story. She was very excited. It was her first time at the ballet. She couldn't wait to see the ballet named *The Nutcracker* for the first time. Jack wished he was at a hockey game instead of the <u>dreary</u> ballet. The lights flickered to signal the show was about the start. The audience hushed. Then, the curtain lifted and dancers gracefully appeared on stage to plié, twirl, jump, and <u>arabesque</u>. It was the most <u>exquisite</u> thing Emily had ever seen. The dancers seemed to float on air. Jack enjoyed the scene where the Nutcracker fights the evil Rat King. Jack and Emily both enjoyed their first ballet experience!

1. In this passage, the word *usher* means

    A. "a bridegroom at a wedding."

    B. "person in a theater who shows people to their seats."

    C. "a door keeper in a court of law."

    D. "an officer who introduces people before they enter a room."

2. What does *program* mean as it is used in the passage?

    A. a radio or television performance or production

    B. a sequence of instructions a computer uses to solve a problem

    C. a planned grouping of activities for a planned purpose like the cheerleading camp program

    D. a list that gives the performers, supporters, music, and performance summary for a show

3. In the passage, *dreary* means the opposite of _____.
    A. *exciting*   B. *boring*   C. *tiring*   D. *bleak*

4. What does *arabesque* mean?

    A. a spiraling image

    B. a pose standing on one leg with one arm in front and one arm and one leg behind

    C. a short piece of music for a piano that is light and dreamy

    D. any decorated object using flowers, fruits, and animals in a fanciful pattern

5. In this passage, the word *exquisite* means

    A. "person who is overly concerned about his outside appearance."

    B. "carefully picked or sought after."

    C. "a rare and special beauty."

    D. "intense pain."

Read the dictionary and thesaurus entry. Answer the questions that follow.

---

e-nor-mous
[e-ˈnor-mus]
adjective
    1 very great in size, number, or degree
    2 archaic: very wicked
    synonym: huge, vast, immense, giant
    antonym: little, wee, tiny, petite, miniature, teeny, microscopic

en-rich
[in-ˈrich]
verb
    1 to make rich or richer
    2 to make more meaningful or rewarding
    3 to add fertilizer to
    4 to add nutrients to
    5 to add to the beauty or character of
    synonym: adorn, decorate, embellish, enhance, fortify, garnish, upgrade, supplement, fertilize
    antonym: deprive, remove, dismantle

---

6. The *e* in the word *enormous* sounds MOST like the *e* in which word?

   A. pet   B. see   C. fetch   D. gentle

7. Which sentence uses *enrich* in the same way as definition number five?

   A. Jake had to enrich the soil before planting corn.

   B. Andrew wanted to enrich his vacation with excitement and fun.

   C. The purchase of stocks enriched Walter's bank account.

   D. The diamond necklace enriched the beauty of the dress.

8. Which guide words might mark this page?

   A. enigma – enroll   C. enrage – enter

   B. enhance – enough   D. engulf – enrage

9. Which definition of the word *enrich* BEST matches how it is used in the sentence below?

       Kyle had to find a multivitamin enriched with calcium.

   A. 1   B. 2   C. 3   D. 4

10. Which word BEST replaces *enormous* in the sentence below?

       Eleanor had an *enormous* crush on Calvin.

   A. wicked   B. huge   C. petite   D. deprive

11. Which word means the opposite of the word *enrich*?

   A. adorn   B. garnish   C. deprive   D. supplement

12. What part of speech is *enormous*?

   A. noun   B. verb   C. adverb   D. adjective

Chapter 3
Word Meanings

This chapter addresses the following GPS-based CRCT standard(s):

> **ELA4R3** The student understands and acquires new vocabulary and uses it correctly in reading and writing. The student
>
> **h.** Recognizes and uses words with multiple meanings (e.g., sentences, school, hard) and determines which meaning is intended from the context of the sentence.
>
> **i.** Identifies and applies the meaning of the terms antonym, synonym, and homophone.

WORDS WITH MULTIPLE MEANINGS

Many words have **more than one meaning**. This means that, if you look them up, you will find more than one definition.

An example is the word *fast*.

Multiple Meanings of *Fast*		
Part of Speech	**Definition**	**Example**
adverb	quickly	He ran fast and won the race. Time seemed to go by fast.
adjective	securely attached	The glue held the model fast. I had to hold fast to the handlebars as I rode down the hill.
adjective	very loyal	They were fast friends.
verb	go without food	The patient had to fast before the operation.

To tell which meaning of a word applies, you have to look at how the word is used. Look around the word at the context (the words around it). The skill of using context clues, which you read about in chapter 2, can help you here. Knowing the many meanings of words will help you to expand your vocabulary. It can also increase your understanding as you read.

Practice 1:   Words with Multiple Meanings

ELA4R3h

Read each sentence. Decide what the underlined word means. Then, find the sentence in which the word in boldface has the same meaning as the underlined word.

1.   Milla used the <u>balance</u> to measure out the chemicals for her science experiment.

   A. Dr. Houser instructed the class to use a **balance** to measure out the sulfur.

   B. Ann had to figure out the **balance** of her checking account.

   C. Our ropes course made us walk across a log in the air, which tested our **balance**.

   D. The chaotic office needed someone with a lot of **balance** to run it smoothly.

2. Our friendship <u>dates</u> from elementary school in Mrs. Reusings' first grade.
   A. The dessert was made with **dates** and walnuts wrapped in a thin pastry.
   B. Two appointments are set for **dates** later this week.
   C. Cheese-making **dates** back as far as 6000 BC.
   D. The **date** on the letter is July 5, 2007.

3. Jane had the <u>habit</u> of biting her lips when she was nervous.
   A. Hallie wore a nun's **habit** for Halloween this year.
   B. Trevor has the **habit** of tapping his foot when he watches TV.
   C. Arthur's fleshy **habit** required him to buy two airline tickets.
   D. The king's royal **habit** was important to his public image.

4. That painting is from the Impressionist <u>Period.</u>
   A. She didn't need a question mark but a **period** at the end of the sentence.
   B. The game wasn't won until the third **period**.
   C. Dinosaurs lived during the Mesozoic **Period**.
   D. Adnon was checked out during first **period** today.

5. Blake was grateful that his friends decided to <u>shower</u> him with help after lightning struck his house.
   A. Today's forecast is for a rain **shower** in the morning and clear skies in the afternoon.
   B. I was eager to **shower** my parents with appreciation for paying off my car loan.
   C. Barbara and Joanie threw a baby **shower** for Connie last week.
   D. Isabella took a **shower** before going to dinner with her friends.

SYNONYMS

A **synonym** is a word that is close in meaning to another word. You can use a thesaurus to find synonyms. As you read in chapter 2, a thesaurus is a dictionary of synonyms and antonyms.

Using synonyms is one way to improve your writing. It gives your writing variety. If you use the same word over and over, you can replace it at times with a word that means the same thing. This keeps your writing from sounding repetitive. Synonyms also help you to improve your vocabulary. Knowing more ways to say something can help you express yourself better.

For example, look at this sentence.

> Mom got <u>mad</u> about all the mud that my dog, Baily, tracked on the carpet.

What is another word that means the same or about the same as *mad*?

   A. funny   B. pale   C. upset   D. tired

If you picked C, you're right! The words *mad* and *upset* and both synonyms for *angry*. Mom might have thought the mud on the carpet was *funny* (but probably not). She also could have gone *pale* or felt *tired* at the thought of cleaning it. But, none of these words mean the same as *mad*.

Practice 2: Synonyms

ELA4R3i

Read sentences 1 through 4. For each one, choose the word that means the same or about the same as the underlined word.

1. The baby <u>wailed</u> with impatience because he was hungry.

   A. whispered   C. shouted

   B. cried   D. moaned

2. The ghost walked down the stairs and <u>vanished</u> right before our eyes.

   A. enlarged   B. shrank   C. disappeared   D. rose

3. The mouse <u>scampered</u> across the floor and under the refrigerator.

   A. ran

   B. walked

   C. limped

   D. crawled

4. The room was so cold that I couldn't stop <u>quivering</u>.
   A. shaking   B. running   C. walking   D. laughing

Read sentences 5 and 6. Notice that each one has repeated words or phrases. Choose a synonym that can replace the underlined word or phrase.

5. He <u>went up</u> the stairs from the basement, and then he went up to the door to see who was there.
   A. approached   B. climbed   C. stood   D. tried

6. She laid her head on a soft pillow to watch the <u>soft</u> colors of the sunset.
   A. harsh   B. bright   C. quiet   D. pastel

ANTONYMS

An **antonym** is a word that means the opposite of another word. For example, *loud* is an antonym of *soft*. And, *running* is an antonym of *standing*. Almost all words have some word that means the opposite or near opposite. Most of the time, you can figure it out without any help, but if you are stuck and need help, antonyms can be found in a thesaurus.

Here is an example. Read this sentence.

    My knees went <u>weak</u> when I saw how high the roller coaster was.

Which word means the opposite of *weak*?

    A. frail   B. strong   C. sick   D. scared

Did you choose B? Good for you! *Strong* is the opposite of *weak*. The word *frail* is actually a synonym for *weak*, so it is not the opposite. Both *sick* and *scared* are ways a person might feel when seeing a very high roller coaster, but neither one means the opposite of *weak*.

Practice 3: Antonyms
ELA4R3i

Read each sentence. Choose the word that means the opposite or nearly the opposite of the underlined word.

1. My grandmother always said that <u>honesty</u> pays off in the end, and it did for me.

   A. lying   B. truth   C. accuracy   D. blundering

2. Some places in a city can be <u>dangerous</u> at night.
   A. cheerful   B. lethal   C. dark   D. safe

3. The mountain seemed <u>enormous</u> to us when we started hiking up it.

   A. giant   C. majestic

   B. tiny   D. monstrous

4. I was very <u>grateful</u> for all the help from my friends after my surgery.

   A. thankful   C. unappreciative

   B. refreshed   D. discontented

5. We didn't realize how cold it was last night until we found the <u>frozen</u> water in the dog's bowl.

   A. gelled   C. hardened

   B. melted   D. thickened

6. My parents have always wanted to see me <u>succeed</u> in life.

   A. fail   B. triumph   C. escape   D. prosper

HOMOPHONES

Have you ever come across a word that sounds like another but has a different meaning? If you have, then you know what a **homophone** is. Homophones are two or more words that sound the same when pronounced but have different meanings and spellings. Not knowing the right homophone to use could lead to lower grades. Below is a chart with some of the most common homophones. Maybe you know other homophones too. Share them with a classmate!

Common Homophones	
Homophones	**Definitions**
aisle	a path between a row of chairs
I'll	contraction for "I will"
allowed	permitted
aloud	spoken normally, as opposed to whispered
ant	an insect
aunt	the sister of your mother or father
bare	uncovered
bear	a furry mammal that hibernates in winter
be	verb meaning "to exist"
bee	flying insect that makes honey
blew	past tense of *blow*
blue	color
board	a plank of wood
bored	feeling uninterested and dull
brake	come to a stop
break	split or crack

buy	purchase
by	near or next to
cent	penny
sent	mailed
scent	odor
deer	mammal that lives in the forest
dear	beloved
flea	small insect
flee	run away
flew	past tense of *fly*
flu	influenza (disease)
flour	white powder for baking
flower	blossom of a plant
for	with the purpose of, opposite of *against*
four	number
hall	passageway
haul	transport
heal	mend, get well
heel	the back part of the foot
he'll	contraction of "he will"
heard	past tense of *hear*
herd	a group of animals, like cows
hole	an opening or hollow
whole	entire, complete
knight	medieval soldier
night	daily period of darkness
knot	made by tying something
not	negative adverb
knows	has knowledge
nose	part of the face through which you smell
new	unused; not old
knew	past tense of *know*

one	number
won	past tense of *win*
pair	two of something
pear	juicy, apple-like fruit
plain	not fancy
plane	airplane
rain	water falling from the sky
reign	time during which a king rules
rein	strap used to control a horse
read	understand words on a page
reed	tall, slender plant; vibrating part of a musical instrument
role	a part played by someone
roll	something tube-shaped; to tumble or rotate
sea	large body of water
see	to perceive with the eyes
sew	to join with a needle and thread
so	conjunction
sow	to plant
son	male child
sun	star that gives the earth light and heat
stair	step
stare	look at for a long time
steal	to take without paying
steel	metal alloy
two	number
to	toward or for
too	also
wail	cry out
whale	large oceanic mammal
way	path or direction
weigh	to measure by weight
weak	not strong
week	seven-day period
would	used for possibilities or polite requests (Would you mind?)
wood	building material made from trees

Practice 4: Homophones

ELA4R3i

Read the sentences. Each one contains several words that have homonyms. One is used incorrectly. Choose the one that doesn't belong.

1. My <u>dear</u> <u>aunt</u> is in Florida <u>for</u> a <u>weak</u>.

   A. dear

   B. aunt

   C. for

   D. weak

2. The big <u>read</u> bird <u>flew</u> down the <u>hall</u> and into <u>our</u> living room.

   A. read

   B. flew

   C. hall

   D. our

3. It <u>reigned</u> so hard all <u>night</u> we couldn't <u>see</u> the <u>road</u>.

   A. reigned   C. see

   B. night   D. road

4. The box of <u>flour</u> <u>weighed</u> so much it threatened to <u>brake</u> the <u>board</u> it sat on.

   A. flour

   B. weighed

   C. brake

   D. board

5. <u>Would</u> anyone <u>know</u> <u>whose</u> <u>genes</u> these are in the laundry basket?

   A. would

   B. know

   C. whose

   D. genes

6. <u>Two</u> <u>mournings</u> this month, <u>he'll</u> be <u>allowed</u> to sleep in.

   A. two

   B. mournings

   C. he'll

   D. allowed

CHAPTER 3 SUMMARY

Many words have **multiple meanings**. To know which meaning is correct, look at how the word is used. Also, use context clues from what is around it.

A **synonym** is a word that is close in meaning to another word. Using synonyms is one way to improve your writing. Use a thesaurus to find synonyms.

An **antonym** is a word that means the opposite of another word. Antonyms also can be found in a thesaurus.

Homophones are two or more words that sound the same but have different meanings and spellings.

CHAPTER 3 REVIEW

ELA4R3h, i

Read the paragraph, and answer the questions that follow.

Golf Basics: What You Really Need to Know

The game of golf is fun. It seems like a simple game of hitting a small ball into a whole in the ground, but it's not. To play, you must learn several basic things. First, you must know how to hold the club correctly. Your grip on the club will affect how you swing the club. Your grip will start with your left hand holding the club loosely with the thumb, thumbnail straight up, on the top of the handle and pointing directly down to the ground. The right hand will interlace the last finger between the first and second finger of the left hand. The right hand will then grip the thumb of the left hand and the golf club loosely with the thumb of the right hand pointing down the club handle and not wrapped around the handle. Next, to master the game of golf, you must learn the swing and stance. It is important to stand in a certain way. This is the most important part to master. With each different club you use, you have to adjust the swing and stance. In golf, you have a bag of clubs called woods, irons, wedges, and putters. There are different levels of each club type. A good golfer knows how to change his swing and stance to use each one of the different clubs to make the ball roll write where he wants it.

---

1. Read the sentence below, and find the homophone that is incorrectly used.

   It <u>seems</u> like a simple game of hitting a small ball into a <u>whole</u> in the ground, but <u>it's</u> <u>not</u>.

   A. seems

   B. whole

   C. it's

   D. not

2. Which word means the opposite of the underlined word in the sentence below?

> To play the game well, you must learn several basic things.

A. behinning

C. advanced

B. introductory

D. elementary

3. Which word means the opposite of the underlined word in the sentence below?

> The right hand will interlace the last finger between the first and second finger of the left hand.

A. join

C. interweave

B. link

D. untangle

4. Which definition is MOST like the meaning of the word *handle* as it is used in the sentence below?

> Your grip will start with your left hand holding the club loosely with the thumb, thumbnail straight up, on the top of the handle and pointing directly down to the ground.

A. responsibility to supervise

C. part grasped by the hand

B. put up with

D. a name or title

5. Which word means the same or about the same as the underlined word in the sentence below?

> Next, to master the game of golf, you must learn the swing and stance.

A. forget

B. learn

C. neglect

D. ignore

6. Which definition fits the meaning of the word *swing* as it is used in the sentence below?

> Next, to master the game of golf, you must learn the swing and stance.

A. jazz played with a steady, pulsing beat

B. a short pass thrown to the back running outside

C. voters who have not made a decision and can be influenced to change their votes

D. to move in a wide arc or circle

7. Which word means the same as the underlined word in the sentence below?

> It is important to stand in a certain way.

A. specific   B. unsure   C. general   D. relaxed

8. Which definition fits the meaning of the word *adjusted* as it is used in the sentence below?

> With each different club you use, you have to adjust the swing and stance.

A. settle   B. adapt   C. regulate   D. save

9. Which word means the opposite of the underlined word in the sentence below?

> There are different levels of each club type.

A. similar   B. individual   C. diverse   D. unusual

10. Read the sentence below, and find the homophone that is incorrectly used.

> A master golfer knows how to change his swing and stance to use each one of the different clubs to make the ball roll write where he wants it.

A. knows   B. one   C. roll   D. write

Chapter 4
Reading for Information

This chapter addresses the following GPS-based CRCT standard(s):

ELA4R1 The student demonstrates comprehension and shows evidence of a warranted and responsible explanation of a variety of literary and informational texts.

For **informational texts**, the student reads and comprehends in order to develop understanding and expertise and produces evidence of reading that:

a. Locates facts that answer the reader's questions.

f. Summarizes main ideas and supporting details.

h. Distinguishes fact from opinion or fiction.

Have you ever read writing that gave you information? Perhaps you read how to do something. Maybe you read a science article about nature or a book for social studies. In every case, reading for information means that you read to learn about a topic. In this chapter, you will practice skills that help you read for information. Let's begin with a look at finding the main idea.

MAIN IDEA

One important skill for reading informational writing is spotting the **main idea**. The main idea is what the writing is about. This idea is the focus of the passage. To identify a main idea, a reader must first read carefully. A good reader will also look for clues and use thinking questions like these:

- What is the passage mostly about?
- Is there one sentence that states the main idea?
- How could I summarize in my own words?

Let's take a look at a sample passage and try to identify the main idea.

> *Tales of a Fourth Grade Nothing* is a novel by Judy Blume. The book was first published in 1972. It tells the tale of Peter Warren Hatcher and his baby brother, Farley. Farley goes by the nickname "Fudge." Fudge is sort of a troublemaker. He gets into mess after mess. Peter has to pick up the pieces. Fudge's naughty behavior seems to bring him attention. On the other hand, Peter is unhappy to play the role of responsible older brother. The story is told from Peter's point of view. Readers everywhere find the story funny and realistic. *Tales of a Fourth Grade Nothing* is an excellent work for young readers.

First, apply the thinking questions to this passage:

- What is the passage mostly about?
- Is there one sentence that states the main idea?
- How could I summarize in my own words?

Now, take a look at the choices below. Choose the sentence that BEST states the main idea.

A. *Tales of a Fourth Grade Nothing* is a novel by Judy Blume.

B. Fudge's naughty behavior seems to bring him attention.

C. The story is told from Peter's point of view.

D. *Tales of a Fourth Grade Nothing* is an excellent work for young readers.

Which one did you choose? If you chose D, then you are correct. That sentence best states the main idea of the passage. This passage informs the reader. It tells the reader about why *Tales of a Fourth Grade Nothing* is a book that young readers would enjoy. The details in the passage help to explain the qualities of the novel that make it fun and interesting to read.

Practice 1: Main Idea

ELA4R1f

Read the passages. Answer the question after each one.

> The American Civil War is an important but sad part of history. It is a sad part of history because many people died. This war was between the southern states and the northern states. It took place from 1861 to 1864. One main cause of the war was the issue of slavery. Slavery created conflict between the states. At the end of the war, the North won. As a result, slavery was officially ended.

1. Which sentence(s) states the main idea?

   A. The American Civil War is an important but sad part of history.

   B. This war was between the southern states and the northern states.

   C. One of the main causes of war was the issue of slavery.

   D. At the end of the war, the North won.

> Many people don't know that the sun is a star. In fact, it is the nearest star to the earth. The sun is about 4.5 billion years old. The sun warms the earth. It supports life on earth. Without the sun, life on earth would not be possible. There is much that people do not know about the sun.

2. Which sentence states the main idea of this paragraph?

   A. In fact, it is the nearest star to the earth.

   B. The sun is about 4.5 billion years old.

   C. The sun warms the earth

   D. There is much that people do not know about the sun.

What does it take for people to live? Humans have several basic needs. One basic need is food. Everyone must eat food to have energy. Another basic need is water. Actually, the human body is made up mainly of water. Shelter is another need. People need to be protected from the sun, rain, wind, and cold. Finally, humans need air and a clean environment.

3. Which sentence states the main idea?

   A. What does it take for people to live?

   B. Humans have several basic needs.

   C. Actually, the human body is made up mainly of water.

   D. Shelter is another need.

What's the best thing to do when the summer rolls around? The summer is a time to have fun, learn, and share with family. One idea for summer is to attend a summer camp. There are day camps, and there are overnight camps. When kids attend overnight camps, they might spend a week or more away from home. These camps offer fun and educational activities. Also, many families have summertime family reunions. Family members from all parts of the country gather in one state. Some kids vacation with families and get to see the sights of the country. Others are at home with friends and family, hanging out in the neighborhood. This is a good option too. There are so many ways that a kid can spend summer vacation. There is no reason for a kid to be bored for the summer.

4. Which of the following sentence(s) states the main idea of this paragraph?

   A. What's the best thing to do when the summer rolls around?

   B. The summer is a time to have fun, learn, and share with family.

   C. One idea for summer is to attend a summer camp.

   D. There is no reason for a kid to be bored for the summer.

SUPPORTING DETAILS

Another part of being a good reader is recognizing important **supporting details**. Supporting details are facts, explanations, and examples. They help to explain and prove the main idea. Without strong supporting details, a main idea is less believable.

You can think of supporting details like part of building a house. If you think of the structure of a house, you usually see a roof at the top. However, without the beams that hold up the structure of the house, the roof would not stay up. In informational writing, the main idea is like the roof. The supporting details are the beams that hold it up.

To determine which details in a passage are supporting details, one must first read carefully to discover the main idea. The next step is to seek out sentences that help explain that idea. These are supporting details. Let's take a look at a sample passage.

> When it was founded in 1977, this TV channel was called Pinwheel. Today, it is called Nickelodeon. It is trusted by many parents. It is thought to be a child-friendly station with clean programs. Nickelodeon now airs a variety of shows. These include learning and action programs. The channel also has many regular sitcoms.

Which main idea statement would BEST be supported by the details of the paragraph?

   A. *Drake and Josh* is a popular sitcom that is aired on the Nickelodeon channel.

   B. Nickelodeon is a favorite of children and approving parents.

   C. Some children are not allowed to watch television.

   D. *The Amanda Show* is also shown on Nickelodeon.

In order to figure this out, you must first ask yourself a thinking question:

- What is the paragraph mostly about?

The paragraph is about the cable channel Nickelodeon. It is not about any specific shows on the network. Rather, it is about Nickelodeon in general. So, we can remove answer choices A and D. You can also eliminate answer C. There is nothing in the paragraph about some children not being allowed to watch TV. B is the best answer choice.

Practice 2: Supporting Details

ELA4R1f

Read each passage. Then, answer the questions that follow.

> Many people now know that recycling is a good idea. In this way, natural resources last for the future. There are many ways to recycle. At school, there are probably bins for used white paper. At the grocery store, you can buy reusable grocery bags. You can even buy tissues or notebook paper made from recycled resources.

1. Which sentence BEST states the main ideas of the details above?

   A. Everyone should recycle plastics.

   B. Recycling is a popular and wise idea today.

   C. Everyone should recycle paper.

   D. People have been recycling for centuries.

> He was the nation's first president. George Washington is often called one of the country's "founding fathers." He was born in Virginia in 1732. He had very little schooling, but he learned skills and trades. He joined the Virginia militia. While in the army, Washington became an officer. Later, he helped create the US Constitution. He was the President of the United States of America from 1789 to 1797.

2. Which sentence BEST states the main idea supported by the details above?

   A. George Washington is on the American one-dollar bill.

   B. George Washington is an important figure in American history.

   C. George Washington was a brilliant military officer.

   D. George Washington has a monument in Washington, D.C.

Smallpox is a deadly disease. It hit North America in the late eighteenth century. Many people became sick. Some even died of smallpox. Today, doctors can cure smallpox.

3. Which sentence BEST states the main idea of the details above?

A. The smallpox vaccination was a very useful and long-awaited scientific discovery.

B. The smallpox epidemic marked a deadly time in the history of North America.

C. Children today in North America get sent home when they have smallpox.

D. Slaves of North American southern states died of smallpox and other diseases.

What is a smart, funny, and friendly gray mammal that lives in the sea? If you said dolphin, then you are correct. Dolphins are sea animals that are known for being friendly and intelligent. They live in shallow sea water and eat small fish. Dolphins are popular with humans.

4. Which sentence BEST states the main idea of the details above?

A. Dolphins, whales, cats, dogs, and goldfish make great pets.

B. Dolphins are fun and interesting, highly intelligent, and good animals for television.

C. A dolphin is a gray, smart, funny mammal that lives in shallow sea water.

D. Flipper is a great name for a pet dolphin, while Lassie is a great name for a pet dog.

FINDING FACTS

Remember, we read informational texts to learn about a topic. Informational texts contain facts. Facts are statements that can be proved true. Facts are not debatable because there is a clear way to prove their truth. A good reader must be able to **identify facts**. Let's take a look at a sample passage.

> Life for slaves in Colonial America was hard and sad. Slaves were expected to work all day. From sunrise to sunset, many slaves had to work in the fields. They tended crops such as cotton. Often, they had to take care of the plantation animals. Slave family bonds were of little value. In many cases, mothers were torn away from their own children. Many slave families were separated. Instead of being respected as humans, many slaves were treated like animals.

How long was the work day for many field slaves?

    A. from nine to five

    B. from noon until midnight

    C. from sunrise to sunset

    D. none of these

Which answer did you choose? If you chose C, then you are correct. By reading carefully, you learn that some field slaves were expected to work from sunrise until sunset.

Practice 3: Finding Facts

ELA4R1a

Read the selections, and answer the questions that follow.

Water is one of the earth's most valuable resources. It is used in many ways. One way that people use water is to make crops grow. These crops then become food for humans. Water also provides food in another way. Fish are found in the water. They are a part of the diets of many people. Water is also used for industry. Many factories and other businesses need water to make products and for cleaning. Finally, water is needed to make electricity. Without electricity, so many conveniences of today's world would not be possible.

1. Which of the following is a way that water is used?

    A. to make crops grow

    B. to help run industries

    C. for hunting

    D. both A and B

2. Water is a _____.

    A. luxury   B. resource   C. waste   D. treasure

In the American Colonial era, laws were different from today. Citizens did not have the right of free speech. This meant that they could not speak badly of the king of England. If they did, they could be charged with a crime. Also, there was public punishment such as lashing or even hangings. Women also had fewer rights than they have today. They were not as free to do as they pleased. Often, women were looked upon as property of their husbands.

3. What right that exists today did not exist during the American colonial era?

    A. the right of free speech

    B. the right of women to marry

    C. the right of public punishment

    D. the right of women to own property

4. Which colonial era practice is no longer in use today?

A. courtroom trial   C. jail

B. public lashing   D. none of these

FACT AND OPINION

Wilson says to his friend, Dominick, "The earth is the third planet from the sun."

Dominick then says to his friend, Wilson, "You are the smartest kid on earth."

- Which one is a fact? Which one is an opinion? Why?

The first statement—"the earth is the third planet from the sun"—is a **fact**. This can be proved true. Scientists and astronomers have researched and know this to be so.

The second statement, however—"you are the smartest kid on earth"—is an **opinion**. It is only what Dominick thinks. There is no way for this statement to be proven true. Dominick doesn't even know every kid on earth. Even if he did, how could he possibly know which kid was absolutely the smartest?

Facts are statements that can be proved true. Opinions are statements that may be based upon facts, but are not able to be proved true. In fact, many opinions are not truths. They are just what people feel/think about something. Let's take a look at some examples.

Facts	Opinions
There are four seasons: spring, summer, winter, and fall.	Summer is the best season of all.
Four quarters make one dollar.	Paper money is better than coins.
Dogs and cats are popular house pets.	Dogs make better pets than cats.

Practice 4: Fact and Opinion

ELA4R1h

Decide whether each statement is a fact or an opinion.

1. Water freezes at thirty-two degrees Fahrenheit.
   A. fact   B. opinion

2. The air in this house feels like it is freezing.
   A. fact   B. opinion

3. Fourth grade is the most important school year.
   A. fact   B. opinion

4. Thomas Jefferson was America's third president.
   A. fact   B. opinion

5. Watching television is a waste of time.
   A. fact   B. opinion

6. Humans are mammals.
   A. fact   B. opinion

Thomas Jefferson

CHAPTER 4 SUMMARY

Reading for information means that you are reading to learn about a topic.

The **main idea** is the focus of the writing. To find the main idea, ask these questions:

What is the passage mostly about?

Is there one sentence that states a main idea?

How can I summarize the passage in my own words?

- **Supporting details** are facts, explanations, and examples that help to explain and prove the main idea statement.

- **Facts** are statements that can be proved true. A good reader can find and **identify facts**.

- **Opinions** are statements that may be based upon facts, but are not able to be proved true.

CHAPTER 4 REVIEW

ELA4R1a, f, h

Read each passage, and answer the questions that follow.

> Settlers from Europe arrived in North America in the sixteenth century. They met Native Americans who lived along the Atlantic coast. The settlers observed the lives of the Native Americans. They found that these people knew many things about the land. Some of their crops were corn, beans, and pumpkins. Other foods they ate included fish, deer, and turkey. Food was plentiful. The area was heavily populated with Native American families. Their many skills helped them to preserve the quality of the land. They would often move to different regions of the coast as the seasons changed. They also moved when resources in one area became less available. In this way, they were able to work with the land and allow each area time to replenish its resources.

1. Which sentence BEST states the main idea of this passage?

    A. Native Americans lived a simple, carefree life.

    B. Europeans learned a great deal from the ways of Native Americans.

    C. Native Americans were sad to see Europeans arrive.

    D. Native Americans had discovered how to make the most of their land.

2. Which of the following is a statement of fact?

    A. Native Americans lived a simple, carefree life.

    B. Europeans enjoyed living among Native Americans.

    C. Native Americans were better off before the Europeans arrived.

    D. The Algonquin Native Americans lived along the Atlantic coast.

3. Which sentence supports the following statement?

> Native Americans had learned many skills that helped them to preserve the quality of the land.

A. When settlers from Europe arrived in North America in the sixteenth century, they met Native Americans.

B. They would often move to different regions of the Atlantic coastal area as the seasons changed.

C. Settlers found that these people had simple ways of life that worked well for them.

D. Other sources of food for the Native Americans included fish and small game.

4. When did settlers from Europe arrive in North America and meet Native Americans along the Atlantic Coast?

A. during the sixteenth century

B. during the seventeenth century

C. during the eighteenth century

D. during the nineteenth century

5. Which of the following is a statement of fact?

A. For Native Americans, life was easygoing, lazy, and slow.

B. Native Americans loved the new European settlers that had traveled across the sea.

C. Settlers from Europe arrived in North America in the sixteenth century.

D. European settlers were friendly and fair to the Native Americans.

Betsy Byars was born in 1928 in Charlotte, North Carolina. She is a children's author who writes realistic fiction. Byars uses the experiences of her life to get ideas for writing. This means that Byars' books often feature her real life hometown. Her books also tell stories that have happened to her or people that she has known. Byars' books are especially known for their humor. Some favorite titles by Betsy Byars are *After the Goat Man, Cracker Jackson,* and *Goodbye, Chicken Little.* She now lives in South Carolina where she continues to write.

6. Where was Betsy Byars born?
   A. Charleston, South Carolina
   B. Savannah, Georgia
   C. Charlotte, North Carolina
   D. Pensacola, Florida

7. Which sentence is BEST supported by the details of the paragraph?
   A. Betsy Byars' novels are often enjoyed by young readers.
   B. Betsy Byars is not a very successful children's writer.
   C. Betsy Byars doesn't enjoy writing anything educational.
   D. none of these

8. Which of the following is a statement of fact?
   A. Betsy Byars was born in 1928.
   B. Betsy Byars is a great author.
   C. Betsy Byars is very smart.
   D. Betsy Byars is a funny writer.

9. Which of the following is a statement of opinion?
   A. Betsy Byars was born in 1928 in Charlotte, North Carolina.
   B. Betsy Byars is one of the greatest writers of children's literature.
   C. Betsy Byars uses some of her life experiences as ideas for her writing.
   D. Betsy Byars now lives in Charleston, South Carolina.

Alice Mead is a children's author who often writes about children living in difficult conditions. Her novel, *Junebug*, tells the story of a ten-year-old boy who wishes for more than what life can offer him. Growing up in the projects is complex. It leaves him with hard choices to make. Another book by Mead is *Dawn and Dusk*. This story is set in Iran. It tells the story of Azad. His life is affected by social and political conflict. The settings featured in Mead's work are not always peaceful, but readers can appreciate the reality of her novels' plots.

10. Which sentence is BEST supported by the details of the paragraph?
   A. Mead's writing reaches out to children in many difficult circumstances.

   B. Mead is a mean, cruel writer who likes to make fun of children's bad lives.

   C. Mead has experienced a lot of the world, but she has never lived in a war torn country.

   D. Mead knows children from different places, so she is able to write about their lives.

11. Which of the following is a statement of opinion?
   A. Alice Mead wrote a novel called *Junebug*.

   B. Alice Mead is a fabulous children's writer.

   C. Alice Mead wrote *Dawn and Dusk*.

   D. Alice Mead writes about children.

12. What is the title of Alice Mead's book that features a young boy who has a home in the projects?
   A. *Junebug*

   B. *Dawn and Dusk*

   C. *Mead's Children*

   D. none of these

Chapter 5
How Information is Organized

This chapter addresses the following GPS-based CRCT standard(s):

> **ELA4R1 The student demonstrates comprehension and shows evidence of a warranted and responsible explanation of a variety of literary and informational texts.**
>
> For **informational texts**, the student reads and comprehends in order to develop understanding and expertise and produces evidence of reading that:
>
> **b.** Identifies and uses knowledge of common textual features (e.g., paragraphs, topic sentences, concluding sentences, glossary).
>
> **d.** Identifies and uses knowledge of common organizational structures (e.g., chronological order, cause and effect).
>
> **e.** Distinguishes cause from effect in context.

In chapter 4, you learned about reading for information. This means you read to learn about a topic. In this chapter, you will learn how writers organize ideas. Let's begin with a look at paragraph parts.

PARTS OF A PARAGRAPH

TOPIC SENTENCE

The **topic sentence** is a very important part of a paragraph. It contains the main idea. Most topic sentences come at the beginning of the paragraph. Let's take a look at an example.

> When having fun in the sun, it is important to protect your skin. One way to protect your skin is to use sunblock. It is a good idea to use sunblock before an afternoon at the pool or the beach. Another way to protect your skin is to wear a hat on very sunny days. There are many fun choices for sun hats. Wearing cool, light-colored fabrics is another way to protect the skin. This fabric will reflect light and keep you cooler. There are many ways to protect the skin while enjoying the sun.

In this paragraph, all of the details are about ways to protect the skin from the sun. Which sentence is the topic sentence? If you said the first sentence, then you are correct.

> When having fun in the sun, it is important to protect your skin.

This sentence states the main idea of the paragraph. All of the other sentences support this topic sentence.

Practice 1: Topic Sentence

ELA4R1b Inf

Read each paragraph, and answer the questions that follow.

> In this book, a boy named Marty finds a dog. Marty names the dog Shiloh and decides to adopt him. Marty soon learns that Shiloh belongs to a mean man. This man, Judd, has been treating the dog poorly. Judd tries to make Marty return the dog to him. Marty's goal is to keep Shiloh away from Judd. This story is full of suspense. It also has a theme of friendship.

1. Which is the BEST topic sentence to go with the details above?

    A. *Shiloh* is a novel that tells a story of courage and friendship.

    B. Because *Shiloh* is set in West Virginia, people from that area will read it.

    C. Phyllis Reynolds Naylor wrote the novel *Shiloh*.

    D. Shiloh is a dog that makes friends with a boy named Marty.

These two men were friends and military officers. They lived in the 1700s. They are known for traveling across the United States. Because of their trip, early America learned about the land and people in the west.

2. Which topic sentence BEST belongs with the details above?

A. The United States was once an unexplored land.

B. Lewis and Clark were early American explorers.

C. Without Lewis and Clark, we would not have explorer games to play.

D. Explorers like Lewis and Clark must be brave and smart.

He was a warrior and chief. Crazy Horse was known for his pride in the Native American way of life. In fact, Crazy Horse was one of the last Native American chiefs to give in to English settlers. Crazy Horse will always be remembered for his bravery and spirit.

3. Which is the BEST topic sentence for the details above?

A. Few people know that Crazy Horse was one of ten children in his family.

B. Crazy Horse was a brave Native American chief who lived in the 1800s.

C. Crazy Horse was the first horse to break away from his master.

D. Crazy Horse was a Native American chief who was jealous and angry.

SUPPORTING DETAILS

Supporting details are also important in a paragraph. They help to explain the main idea. They support the topic sentence. Let's look at some examples.

It is very important to maintain a healthy diet. Having a healthy diet means eating a variety of foods. It also means eating fruits and vegetables daily. There are many benefits to eating healthy. One is that it keeps the body strong. For this and other reasons, everyone should try hard to eat healthy foods.

This paragraph is about having a healthy diet. The details of the paragraph all support this idea. If you were to add another sentence to the paragraph as a supporting detail, which of the following would you choose?

A. Exercising can be fun and healthy.

B. Most people don't eat healthy foods every day.

C. Drinking plenty of water is also part of a healthy diet.

D. Many people like fast food, such as pizza and burgers.

If you choose the third sentence, then you are correct.

> Drinking plenty of water is also part of a healthy diet.

Only this sentence could be a supporting detail. It helps to explain the main idea. The other answers are about other topics. They are related but not closely enough to support this main idea.

Practice 2: Supporting Details
ELA4R1b Inf

Read the passage, and then answer the questions that follow.

There are many interesting facts to know about whales. Whales are huge mammals that live in the sea. There are many species of whales. The largest whale is the blue whale. Even though whales live underwater, they breathe. In fact, whales 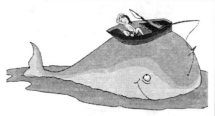 have special lungs. These lungs allow them to hold their breath for long periods of time. This is how they are able to swim underwater without constantly coming up for air. At one time, people hunted and killed whales. People now know a lot about whales, but there is much more to learn.

1. Which sentence would BEST support the information in the paragraph?

A. It would be a great adventure to ride on the back of a whale.

B. Some people say that a man can survive in the belly of a whale.

C. Whales have long life spans, living for thirty years or much more.

D. Blue whales are scary to see in real life because they are so big.

The summer is a great time to connect with family and friends. Many families enjoy having summer barbecues. At a barbecue, there are two main goals: to eat and to have a good time. There is usually great music playing. Family and friends laugh and talk. Kids run about and play. If the barbecue is at a park, the guests may fill the basketball courts while little girls Double Dutch. Hot dogs, hamburgers, ribs, chicken, and side dishes are all on the menu. These barbecues are a fun part of summer.

2. Which sentence would be the BEST supporting information to add to this paragraph?

    A. Basketball is a sport that is enjoyed by many, while Double Dutch is enjoyed by a few.

    B. Many people have their own grills, some of which use charcoal and some gas.

    C. There will also be dishes such as potato salad and sweet treats like apple pie.

    D. Some people who are vegetarians will not agree with eating hot dogs or hamburgers.

Childhood is a time of learning and adventure. Many children grow to be taller than their parents. During childhood, people learn the rules of life. People learn to love and respect one another. People also learn their likes and dislikes. Childhood is a time to explore the world. It gives people the chance to find a place in the world and be happy.

3. Which sentence in the paragraph does NOT relate to the topic?

    A. Many children grow to be taller than their parents.

    B. During childhood, people learn the rules of life.

    C. People learn to love and respect one another.

    D. Childhood is a time to explore the world.

> A fun outdoor activity is kite flying. Kites were invented in China but are popular around the world today. Many modern day inventions can be traced back to China. Kites come in various shapes and sizes. They are usually made from paper or fabric. When you are looking for a cool way to spend a windy day, try flying a kite.

4. Which sentence in the paragraph does NOT relate to the topic?

A. A fun outdoor activity is kite flying.

B. Kites were invented in China, but are popular around the world today.

C. Many modern day inventions can be traced back to China.

D. None of these

CONCLUDING SENTENCE

Concluding sentences are also important in a paragraph. Usually, they are found at the very end of the paragraph. These sentences summarize and wrap up the main ideas. Let's take a look at a sentence that concludes this paragraph.

> Amelia Earhart was just a ten-year-old girl when she saw her first plane. Little did she know that she would one day become the first woman to fly across the Atlantic Ocean. She also broke other flying records. When Earhart lived, women were not as free to do some things as they are today. This made flying planes an unlikely career for her. Through hard work and determination, Earhart was able to one day make her dreams come true.

This paragraph is about Amelia Earhart and her amazing deeds as a female pilot. Look at the sentences below. Which do you think would make the best closing sentence for this paragraph?

A. Amelia Earhart was very fashionable as she flew.

B. Amelia Earhart was a good housekeeper and mother also.

C. Amelia Earhart was a pioneer woman and pilot.

D. Amelia Earhart should have lived like other woman of her era.

If you chose C, then you are correct. This sentence best captures and wraps up the main idea of the paragraph.

Practice 3: Concluding Sentence

ELA4R1b Inf

> Harriet Tubman was a courageous woman who lived during the time of slavery. In fact, she was a slave. However, she did not let that stop her from doing great things in her life. As a young woman, she escaped from slavery. She then dedicated her life to others. She rescued many other slaves and worked to end slavery.

1. What is the BEST closing sentence for the paragraph?

   A. Harriet Tubman's escape from slavery must have been difficult.

   B. Harriet Tubman was a brave woman with strength and determination.

   C. Harriet Tubman never did get over her life as a slave; she was always depressed.

   D. Harriet Tubman even became a Union spy during the Civil War.

> Have you ever been to a zoo and seen a huge furry bear that happened to be white? Chances are, you have. That was a polar bear. Polar bears live in the Arctic. They are the top predators there. Their heavy fur protects them from the extreme cold. Sadly, today, polar bears are an endangered species. This means that there are very few left in the wild. Due to human presence in their environment and other factors, polar bears are having a difficult time at survival.

2. What is the BEST closing sentence for the paragraph?

    A. Polar bears are so lovable that they have been in television commercials.

    B. Polar bears are mean and aggressive creatures.

    C. Polar bears and brown bears are from the same family tree.

    D. Polar bears will become extinct if humans do not help them to survive.

> Can you imagine a time in America when people did not have cars? Cars were not used in many places until 1908. That's when Henry Ford's Model T became popular. It was much different than the cars used today. But it started America down the road to driving.

3. What is the BEST closing sentence for the paragraph?

    A. Without the invention of the Model T, imagine what life might be like today.

    B. The Ford Model T was a great invention, but a better invention was the light bulb.

    C. Companies such as Honda, Toyota, and Saturn came along much later.

    D. Detroit, Michigan, is known for many things other than Ford automobiles.

> Many children know the names Big Bird, Ernie, and Oscar. These creatures are called Muppets. They are part of the cast of *Sesame Street*. *Sesame Street* is a TV show that began in 1969. It is loved by many American children. Kids learn the alphabet and numbers from funny Muppet characters.

4. What is the BEST closing sentence for the paragraph?

    A. Some children find the characters too scary to watch.

    B. *Sesame Street* is only an imaginary place.

    C. *Sesame Street* is both fun and educational.

    D. There are many ways to get to *Sesame Street*.

OTHER FEATURES OF TEXT

Sometimes, when you read informational texts, you will notice other features. These features help guide you through what you are reading. Let's take a look at some of them.

TITLE

Many passages and articles have **titles**. The chapters of informational books also have titles. By reading the title, you learn right away about the subject of that chapter. A good title gives you a clue about what you will read. Let's take a look at an example.

> Kool-Aid is a soft drink powder. It was invented in 1927. Since then, children have been enjoying this delicious drink. Parents love the easy recipe. It calls for a packet of Kool-Aid, water, and sugar. Then, *viola*! Some parents even add in a little fruit. What a treat! Kids enjoy the fruity flavors. It is also fun to mix packets and invent new flavors. Kool-Aid is a popular drink.

This passage is about the popularity of Kool-Aid. Look at the choices below and see which one would be a good title for this passage.

A. Kool-Aid: A Small Packet that Packs a Big Punch

B. Kool-Aid: A Great Way to Start Every Day

C. Kool-Aid Stands: A Great Way to Make Money

D. Kool-Aid: It's Better Than Water

If you chose the first title, you are correct.

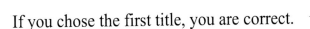

Kool-Aid: A Small Packet that Packs a Big Punch

This title is the best one to let the reader know the subject of the passage.

TABLE OF CONTENTS

Another feature of informational writing is the **table of contents**. A table of contents is a list of chapters that readers will find in a book. It is good to use this tool to know where to find information in a book. Here is a sample table of contents for a book about becoming a better writer.

In what chapter would you find some tips about how to get started as a writer? If you answered chapter 3, then you are correct.

In which chapter might you read about Betsy Byars, who has written over sixty novels for young readers? If you answered chapter 2, then you are correct.

HEADINGS AND SUBHEADINGS

Headings and **subheadings** are like titles. They are labels for sections of writing. Headings and subheadings often break up chapters into smaller parts. This makes the information easier to read. They give the reader clues about what's coming next. In a history book, one chapter may be about the American Civil War. One heading might be "Heroes of War." A subheading in this section might be "Heroes of the Union Army." A reader can skim and easily spot details.

GLOSSARY

A **glossary** is like a dictionary found at the back of a book. The words in a glossary are words that are important to what is written in the book. As in a dictionary, the words are listed in alphabetical order. Each word has a definition. Below is a sample section of a glossary from a math book.

> **Acute angle** An acute angle is any angle that measures less than 90°.
> **Angle** An angle is made up of two rays with a common endpoint.
> **Area** The number of square units inside a figure is the area.

INDEX

An **index** is also found at the back of a book. You will find an index in most textbooks. It lists topics found in the book. Entries in an index are arranged in alphabetical order. Next to each topic are page numbers on which more information can be found. Take a look at a sample segment from the index of a math textbook.

Addition

    of decimals 59–62, 86

    estimating sums, 54–55, 188–191

    of fractions, 193–196, 226, 540

Angles

    adjacent, 292

    central 314, 316, 318

Practice 4:   Other Features of Text

ELA4R1b Inf

Why is there a national spelling bee? Why do people like to spell? Spelling has not always been popular. At one time, no one cared about it. People were not involved. How did this change? America held its first national bee in 1925. This really got people interested. Spelling bees are now very popular. Schools even hold their own. America's annual national spelling bee is in May. Spellers from all over come to compete.

---

1. What would be a good title for this passage?

    A. Spelling Bees and Other Insects

    B. The National Spelling Bee

    C. Spelling is Fun

    D. Math and Spelling

> Many cities use rapid transit. This is a way for people to travel around the city. They do not need cars. City trains are an example. There are also buses and trolleys. Large numbers of people travel at one time. It is usually affordable. Sometimes using rapid transit is faster or a better idea than driving a car. It allows people to move quickly. It also helps with city traffic and pollution.

2. What would be a good title for this passage?
   A. How to Get Around the City
   B. The Best Car for the City
   C. The Benefits of Rapid Transit
   D. Taxis in the City

3. Details on which of the following is MOST LIKELY to be found under the heading "Great Females" in a chapter called "Famous Americans"?
   A. George Washington
   B. Susan B. Anthony
   C. airplanes and cars
   D. sports and other activities

4. Which subheading would MOST LIKELY be found under the heading "Early American Presidents"?
   A. The White House
   B. George Bush
   C. Capitol Hill
   D. George Washington

5. Which of the following is true according to the glossary entry for *sum*?

   > <u>Sum</u> is the total amount of two or more numbers added together.

   A. The sum of 2 and 3 is one.
   B. The sum of 2 and 3 is five.
   C. The sum of 2 and 3 is six.
   D. none of these

6. Which glossary entry would come first?
   A. addition
   B. arithmetic
   C. angle
   D. acute angle

For questions 7 and 8, use this sample from a math book index.

> **Subtraction**
>
>   of decimals 59–62, 86
>
>   estimating differences, 54–55, 188–191
>
>   of fractions, 193–196, 226, 540
>
> **Sum**
>
>   *See addition.* 136

7. On what page(s) would a reader find information on estimating differences?
   A. 54–55   B. 59–62   C. 540   D. none of these

8. On what page would a reader find information about sums?
   A. 59–62   B. 136   C. 226   D. all of these

ORGANIZATION

To help with reading for information, writers often use patterns. These patterns organize ideas. Let's take a look at some patterns.

CAUSE AND EFFECT

The **cause and effect** pattern explores the relationships between ideas or events. It has two basic parts: a cause and an effect. A **cause** makes something happen. The **effect** is what happens as a result. This pattern helps to organize ideas. Cause and effect also is used to organize ideas and to solve problems. You can see the relationship between things. Then, you can find the solution to a problem. Let's look at an example.

> Centuries ago, there lived a large bird that did not fly. This bird, which was a cousin of the pigeon and dove, was called the dodo bird. In the seventeenth century, humans came to the island where these birds were found. The dodo birds then faced a problem. They were hunted and killed by humans. They were also hunted and killed by animals such as dogs and pigs. Humans brought these new animals to the habitat of the dodo. As a result of the humans and new animals on their island, dodo birds became extinct.

This cause and effect paragraph is about the dodo bird and why it became extinct. The cause given is arrival of humans on the island. The effect is the extinction of the dodo birds.

CHRONOLOGICAL

When writers use a chronological pattern, ideas are presented in time order. Let's look at an example.

> Georgia has an interesting history. English settlers founded the colony in the 1700s. In years to come, the state grew quickly. In the 1800s, Georgia was a part of the Civil War. After the war, there was the hard job of rebuilding. The early 1900s were rough years. There were many poor people. Relations between the races were not good. In the mid-1900s, there were many civil rights battles. Today, Georgia has more than four million people. It is a thriving and beautiful state.

This paragraph is about Georgia's history. Notice that all of the details are in time order—from the earliest to the latest.

COMPARISON AND CONTRAST

Comparison and contrast order points out similarities and differences. To compare means to show how things are alike. To contrast means to show how they are different. Let's take a look at an example.

> Dogs and cats are two common house pets. People love both dogs and cats. In general, many pet owners agree that dogs tend to be friendlier than cats. Dogs often seek to please their owners. They want to be near their masters. Cats, on the other hand, are happy to be left alone most of the time. Both dogs and cats have been known to bite and attack. However, since dogs are much stronger, larger creatures, their bites and attacks are often more dangerous. Whether you are a dog or a cat lover, chances are, there's a perfect house pet out there for you.

This paragraph points outs similarities—ways that dogs and cats are alike. It also points out differences between dogs and cats. So, this passage both compares and contrasts.

QUESTION AND ANSWER

Question and answer is another way that writers organize information. Questions are asked and answered in a paragraph. Let's look at an example.

> How do fourth graders spend free time? Reading? Watching TV? Drawing? One popular answer is playing video games. In fact, some kids like playing video games more than playing outdoors. Riding bikes and skateboarding are often second choices to video gaming. Sometimes, homework and chores are pushed aside. Some parents are fine with their kids' love of video games. Others worry that it takes up too much time. Either way, video games are here to stay.

As you can see, this paragraph asks about how fourth graders spend free time. Then, it answers the question.

Practice 5: Organization

ELA4R1d, e Inf

For questions 1 through 5, decide what kind of organization is used in each paragraph.

> Do you know what your body's largest organ is? The heart? Your lungs? No, it's neither of those. Have you thought about your skin? The skin is your body's largest organ. The skin is a living organ and protects the body from germs and disease.

1. What kind of organization is used in the paragraph?

   A. cause and effect

   B. chronological

   C. comparison and contrast

   D. question and answer

Most people have two basic routines. There is one routine for weekdays. There is another for the weekend. For kids, weekdays mean school days. Most kids get up early and get ready for school. They go to school for most of the day. Afterwards may be an activity, homework, dinner, and family. On the weekend, there is also a routine. However, on the weekend, the routine is different. Many kids enjoy sleeping in or watching Saturday morning cartoons. There is also more time for family, friends, and play. Time is usually less formal or structured. Some kids may also attend church, mosque, or synagogue on the weekend.

2. What kind of organization is used in the paragraph?
   A. cause and effect
   B. chronological
   C. comparison and contrast
   D. question and answer

Where did America begin? What was the first successful colony in the New World? It was on May 14, 1607. That's when settlers from Europe founded the first lasting colony in North America. It was called Jamestown. It was a good place to settle because it could be easily defended. But it had some drawbacks. Mosquitoes were a problem. Also, drinking water was not available.

3. What kind of organization is used in the paragraph?
   A. cause and effect
   B. chronological
   C. comparison and contrast
   D. question and answer

Helen Keller was born in Alabama on June 27, 1880. When she was not yet two years old, she became sick. The sickness left Helen deaf and blind. As a child, she learned to communicate using a kind of sign language. In 1886, Helen's mother began looking for someone to help Helen. They soon found Anne Sullivan, who became Helen's tutor.

4. What kind of organization is used in the paragraph?
   A. cause and effect
   B. chronological
   C. comparison and contrast
   D. question and answer

Pollution hurts the earth. It harms humans. It also hurts animals. Cars and factories create smog. Smog makes it hard to breathe. Sometimes, people spill oil into the oceans. Then, ocean animals die. Humans and animals suffer without clean air and water. Pollution can be deadly.

5. In this paragraph, what is it that causes harm to humans and animals?
   A. pollution   B. cars   C. oceans   D. water

For question 6, decide what the correct order of the sentences should be.

(1) Wilbur Wright was born in 1867. (2) To do so, they spent time studying flight. (3) In 1903, the Wright brothers made the first plane. (4) Orville Wright was born in 1871. (5) The brothers wanted to fly.

6. What should be the correct order of the sentence above?
   A. 1,4,5,2,3   C. 1,2,3,4,5

   B. 2,4,5,1,3   D. 3,4,2,5,1

For question 7, read the paragraph. Then, choose the best concluding sentence.

It is easy to use time wisely after school. Be sure to pack the books you need for homework. When you are finished, enjoy the evening. First, when you get home, chat with your family and have a snack. Next, gather your study materials and books. Then, get started on homework. Work on the hardest subject first. After the hardest work is done, finish the assignments in order from the hard ones to the easiest ones. Be sure to eat a healthy, balanced supper.

7. Which of these sentences should come at the end?
   A. When you are finished, enjoy the evening.
   B. Work on the hardest subject first.
   C. Next, gather your study materials and books.
   D. Be sure to pack the books you need for homework.

CHAPTER 5 SUMMARY

The **topic sentence** is a very important part of a paragraph. It contains the main idea. Most topic sentences come at the beginning of the paragraph.

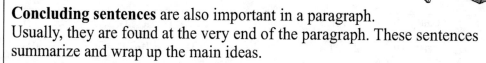

Supporting details are also important in a paragraph. They help to explain the main idea. They support the topic sentence.

Concluding sentences are also important in a paragraph. Usually, they are found at the very end of the paragraph. These sentences summarize and wrap up the main ideas.

Many passages, articles, and informational books have **titles**. By reading the title, you learn right away about the subject of the writing. A good title gives you a clue about what you will read.

Another feature of informational writing is the **table of contents**. A table of contents is a list of chapters that readers will find in a book. It is good to use this tool to know where to find information in a book.

Headings and **subheadings** are like titles. They are labels for sections of writing. Headings and subheadings help make large chunks of information easier to read. They give you clues about what's coming next.

A **glossary** is like a dictionary found at the back of a book. The words in a glossary are words that are important to what is written in the book. As in a dictionary, the words are listed in alphabetical order. Each word has a definition.

An **index** is also found at the back of a book. It lists topics found in the book. Entries in an index are arranged in alphabetical order. Beside each topic, a reader sees all of the page numbers on which information can be found.

The **cause and effect** pattern explores the relationships between ideas and events. A cause is what makes something happen. An effect is what happens.

When writers use a **chronological** pattern, ideas are presented in time order.

Comparison/contrast writing points out similarities and differences. To compare means to show how things are alike. To contrast means to show how things are different.

In the **question and answer** pattern, questions are asked and answered in a paragraph.

CHAPTER 5 REVIEW

ELA4R1b, d, e Inf

For questions 1 through 4, read the passage, and choose the best answer.

> Even as a fourth grader, you can do simple things to be smart with your dollars. For one thing, always save a little. A piggy bank is a simple option for setting aside a little money from allowances or holiday gifts. Make wise use of the money that you do spend. Before you buy something, always think twice.

1. Which topic sentence BEST belongs with the details above?

    A. Saving money can be fun for fourth graders.

    B. It is never too early to start managing your money

    C. Saving money makes you a smart kid.

    D. Why would fourth graders want to save money?

2. Which sentence would BEST support the information in the paragraph?

    A. Many kids do not get much money to spend or save.

    B. Most parents feel that their children are not responsible.

    C. It's great to have a little money saved when you really need it.

    D. There are so many tempting gifts and gadgets to buy.

3. What is the BEST closing sentence for this paragraph?

    A. Being smart with your money now will make you happy later.

    B. A fourth grader is too young to think about saving money.

    C. There are so many great summer vacation activities that cost money.

    D. There is no reason to think about managing money.

4. What would be a good title for this passage?

    A. Ways to Save Summer Money

    B. Being Smart about Your Money

    C. Why Think about Money?

    D. You Can Make Money Everywhere

For questions 5 through 7, use the sample table of contents from a book called "How to Have a Great School Year."

Chapter 1 Starting the Year Strong	2
Chapter 2 Getting Organized	12
Chapter 3 Studying	25
Chapter 4 When to Ask for Help	38
Chapter 5 Achieving Success	45

5. In which chapter would a reader find information about how to set up binders for each class?

    A. Chapter 1

    B. Chapter 2

    C. Chapter 3

    D. Chapter 4

6. Chapter 4 is called "When to Ask for Help." Which of the following would MOST likely be a heading in this chapter?

    A. Doing Homework

    B. Taking Study Breaks

    C. Taking Notes

    D. Finding a Tutor

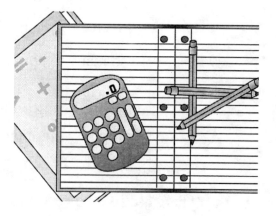

7. In the chapter called "Studying," which of the following would MOST likely be a subheading under a heading "Studying at Home"?

   A. Taking Notes

   B. Using the Library

   C. Finding a Quiet Place

   D. Thinking Ahead

8. Which of the following is true according to the glossary entry for *triangle*?

   Triangle A triangle is a geometric figure having three angles and three sides.

   A. A triangle cannot have four sides.

   B. A square can also be a triangle.

   C. A rectangle can sometimes be a triangle.

   D. A circle can sometimes be a triangle.

For questions 9 and 10, use the sample index from the book called "How to Have a Great School Year."

Studying
at home 5, 17, 26–30
study buddies 35, 39–41
tools 56–58
Taking notes
format 46, 47
Tools 21, 27

9. On what page(s) would a reader find information about different formats for note taking?

   A. 46, 47   C. 5, 17, 26–30

   B. 21, 27   D. none of these

10. On what page(s) would a reader find information about how to choose good friends for study?

A. 56–58

B. 46, 47

C. 35, 39–41

D. none of these

> It can be tempting to be lazy. Playing games is more fun than getting homework done. Also, there are so many entertaining shows to watch. It is hard to turn off the television. Neglecting school work can cause some bad things to happen. Not studying for tests and quizzes can lead to low scores and failing. Besides, when you don't do your best, you disappoint your parents, your teachers, and even yourself.

11. What kind of organization is used in the paragraph?

A. cause and effect

B. chronological

C. comparison and contrast

D. question and answer

> Why do teachers assign summer reading? Isn't summer a time for relaxing and having fun in the sun? Well, summer is a great time to get out and do fun things. However, reading can be fun too. There are many great books out there. You can start with a list from your local library or go online for a look at some great listings for fourth graders.

12. What kind of organization is used in the paragraph?

A. cause and effect

B. chronological

C. comparison and contrast

D. question and answer

Chapter 6
Predictions and Conclusions

This chapter addresses the following GPS-based CRCT standard(s):

> **ELA4R1 The student demonstrates comprehension and shows evidence of a warranted and responsible explanation of a variety of literary and informational texts.**
>
> For **informational texts**, the student reads and comprehends in order to develop understanding and expertise and produces evidence of reading that:
>
> **g.** Makes perceptive and well-developed connections.

In this chapter, you will practice skills that help you when reading. In particular, you will work on making predictions and conclusions. We will begin with making predictions.

MAKING PREDICTIONS

Think about the last movie you watched with friends or family. How did it end? What about the last book you read? As you read the details of the story or watched the action of the movie, did you know what would happen next? Did you try to guess? If so, you were making **predictions**. Making a prediction means guessing what will happen next. To make predictions, readers use what they learn from details in the story and add it to what they already know. Let's take a look at an example.

Jeremiah didn't like to wear dress pants. It was pure torture. For him, it was worse than liver Thursdays. When his mom had announced that the family was going out for a nice dinner, Jere knew this meant that wearing dress pants might be a part of the deal. Why couldn't jeans and comfy cotton shirts go with him everywhere in life? Better yet, what was more comfortable than sneakers and sweats? When Jere got home from school that day, he ran to his room to drop off his backpack. Freezing in his tracks, Jere looked over to the bed where his mother had laid out an outfit for him to wear. When he saw the dress pants, shirt, and tie, his heart sank. Then, his mind kicked into action…

Now, it is time to make a prediction. Based on what you have read so far, what do you think happens next? Take a minute to chat with a partner about this.

Now, look at the choices below. Which of the following seems MOST likely to happen next in the story?

1. Jeremiah will decide it's better to wear slacks than to stay at home and eat liver.

2. Jeremiah will see that he has been silly; wearing slacks is not so bad.

3. Jeremiah will try to figure out some way to get out of wearing slacks.

4. Jeremiah's mom will come in and give him a new choice of clothes to wear.

If you chose the third choice, you are correct. Based on what has happened so far, it is most likely that Jeremiah will try to figure out a way to get out of wearing the slacks.

Practice 1: Making Predictions
ELA4R1g Inf

Savannah was excited. Tonight was Tuesday, and it was her friend Tanya's birthday. She would do homework and then head next door for Tanya's small party. It was Spanish work first, then social studies. By the time she had finished with Ms. Warner's long social studies assignment, it was already quarter to six. Where had the time gone? The party would start at six! "Hmmm," Savannah thought, "I still haven't studied for that math test. If I don't study...." Just then, she heard her mom calling to her from downstairs. It seemed that Tanya was in the living room and had come over to walk Savannah next door. Savannah knew that she should study, but it was just too tempting to get to the party right away. She packed up her school books and hurried downstairs.

"Savannah, have you finished all of your homework, dear?" her mom asked. Nodding her head yes, Savannah hurried out the door hand-in-hand with Tanya.

1. Which of the following seems MOST likely to happen later in the story?

   A. Savannah will return home and get back to studying.

   B. Savannah will not do so well on her math test.

   C. Savannah and Tanya will study during the party.

   D. Savannah's mother will help her with the test.

Michael hurried to school. He had overslept, and now he was late. He worried that Ms. Harris would be angry. He worried that he had forgotten his homework. He worried that he had dropped his right mitten somewhere behind him. Still, he just had to get to school.

Huffing and puffing, he burst through the classroom door. It started at first with Priscilla and then spread across the room. With horror, Michael realized that his classmates were all laughing and pointing. Looking down, he realized why he was the big joke. In his hurry to get to school, Michael had forgotten to trade his pajama bottoms for his blue jeans.

2. Which of the following seems MOST likely to happen next?

A. Michael will begin to sing and dance.

B. Ms. Harris will quiet the class and help Michael.

C. The class will think this is some new fashion.

D. Michael will discover his blue jeans are in the hall.

It was a bright sunny Saturday morning. Kenya and Parker were headed to the neighborhood playground. Kenya's puppy, Sniggle, trailed behind them. Kenya and Parker were friends from school. They were both in Mr. Payne's fourth grade class. Today, they were going to try out the new monkey bars that had just been set up last week. As they reached the playground, the pair noticed something. There was no one there. Usually, on a day like today, there would be at least twenty kids on the playground by now. Something was wrong. They did not want to be in the empty playground alone.

3. Which of the following seems most likely to happen next?

   A. Kenya and Parker will go on and play on the playground.

   B. Sniggle will tell Kenya and Parker why the playground is empty.

   C. Kenya and Parker will not play on the playground.

   D. Sniggle will protect Kenya and Parker while they play.

Leslie and Akira had been best friends since preschool. They had sat side by side and learned to read in Ms. Falcon's first grade class. They were in the same math group when they learned to multiply in Mr. Houston's second grade class. Now, as Leslie and Akira stood side by side on the stage as part of the school spelling bee, they were no longer on the same team. In fact, only one of them could win. As Leslie thought about this, she heard Principal Harper call the next word. It was for Akira. "Spell *disenchantment*," he said. Leslie went pale. She knew how to spell the word. If Akira got it wrong, Leslie could win. She could win and be the school spelling bee champion. Seconds passed slowly as Leslie listened for Akira's answer. There was only silence. Akira didn't know the answer!

4. Which of the following seems MOST likely to happen next?

   A. Akira and Leslie will both spell the word together.

   B. Principal Harper will call it a tie so that friends don't compete.

   C. Leslie will win the spelling bee, and Akira will be happy for her.

   D. Akira will get the spelling of the word from the audience.

The sound of the school fire alarm was louder than a math center that day. Immediately, the children got quiet and listened for instructions from the teacher. "This is not a drill," they all heard a steady voice announce over the school intercom.

5. Which of the following seems MOST likely to happen next?

A. The voice on the intercom will announce that it is all a joke.

B. The students will quickly and quietly exit the school.

C. The teacher will have the students complete math work.

D. The students will put together an exit plan.

Samantha clicked off the television and headed to the kitchen for a snack. As she rummaged around in the cabinet, she couldn't decide what to choose. Snack crackers or snack cakes? Just then, she heard Missy, the family Labrador barking wildly. Samantha went to the window to see what the matter was.

6. Which of the following seems MOST likely to happen next?

A. Samantha will figure out what snack she wants.

B. Samantha will see a cat running through the yard.

C. Missy will be eating Samantha's snack crackers and cakes.

D. Samantha will decide it is a good time to nap.

DRAWING CONCLUSIONS

Another skill that is important for readers is the ability to draw **conclusions**. Drawing a conclusion means to form an opinion. In order to do so, you use facts from what you read. You also use what you already know. Let's take a look at an example.

> The year is 1733. A man settles a city on the coast of Georgia. The man is James Oglethorpe. The city is called Savannah. Savannah is one of the first American cities. It also becomes the very first capital of Georgia. Land in Savannah is marshy. It is also flat. Winters there are mild. Today, Savannah is an important seaport. People come from all over to visit.

Based upon the passage, which of the following statements is MOST likely true?

A. Savannah is a small, quiet town.

B. Savannah is a popular vacation area.

C. Savannah has only brand new buildings.

D. Savannah has tall mountains and winter snow.

If you chose the second statement, then you are correct. Based upon the details in the passage, this is the best response.

Practice 2: Drawing Conclusions

ELA4R1g Inf

Read each passage. Then, answer the questions that follow.

> October 29, 1929, is known as Black Tuesday. On this day, the stock market crashed, and the Great Depression began in the United States. For the next few years, times were very hard. Construction and farming slowed down. Trade between countries also slowed down. Many families had a hard time surviving.

1. Based upon the passage, which of the following is MOST likely true?

    A. During the Great Depression, many families were very wealthy.

    B. During the Great Depression, many families were very poor.

    C. During the Great Depression, many people bought new clothes.

    D. During the Great Depression there were many new inventions.

[Apollo mission photo?]

> On July 20, 1969, a remarkable event happened. The world was watching. On this day, Neil Armstrong was the commander of the *Apollo 11*. This spaceflight was the first to land a man on the moon.

2. Based upon the passage, which of the following is MOST likely true?

    A. Neil Armstrong was the first person to walk on the moon.

    B. The *Apollo 11* probably never made it to the moon.

    C. Neil Armstrong probably never made it to the moon.

    D. none of these

> Ally sat on the porch looking sad. She had no one to play with today. Ever since her best friend Cristina had moved away, Ally was left to entertain herself after school every day. It was no fun playing tag, hide-and-seek, or sharing secrets if you had to do them alone. As she sat, she looked around for an idea, a friend, anything. Just then, she heard something that made her face brighten.

3. Based upon the passage, which of the following is MOST likely true?

    A. Ally heard the voice of a friend calling to her.

    B. Ally heard her favorite song playing in the distance.

    C. Ally's mom was calling her in for dinner.

    D. Ally saw her dog walking across the street.

It was the first day of summer break. Sandy and Bridget were spending the day at the beach with Grandpa. As always, Grandpa was willing to spoil the girls. He bought them ice cream, popcorn, cotton candy, hotdogs, and pizza in less than an hour. While it was fun to enjoy, the girls soon began to feel ill.

4. Based upon the passage, which of the following is MOST likely true?

   A. The girls are ill from too much excitement.

   B. The girls feel ill from too much junk food.

   C. The girls feel ill because it is too hot today.

   D. The girls feel ill because they are tired.

Before America was settled, there was conflict over the land. English settlers and Native Americans fought over territory. In 1838 and 1839, something major happened. Andrew Jackson, the president at that time, ordered Native American tribes to be moved from their land. These Native Americans were moved eight hundred miles west, away from their homes. Many died and suffered along the way. This event is called the Trail of Tears.

5. Based upon the passage, which of the following is MOST likely true?

Trail of Tears

   A. The Native Americans were happy to move away from their land.

   B. English settlers were right to cause this Trail of Tears.

   C. The Native Americans were unhappy to move away from their land.

   D. English settlers decided to let the Native Americans return.

> The Middle Passage was a part of the Atlantic slave trade. The term Middle Passage refers to the trip made by African slaves to the new world. The slaves were stolen from their homelands and packed tightly into ships to sail across the sea. Many slaves died during the voyage. Many others became very ill.   [old ship at sea?]

6. Based upon the passage, which of the following is MOST likely true?

   A. The Middle Passage was a sad and difficult time.

   B. Many Africans were happy to be a part of the Middle Passage.

   C. Many people didn't buy slaves, so Africans were allowed to go home.

   D. none of these

CHAPTER 6 SUMMARY

Making a prediction means to guess what will happen next. To make predictions, you use what you learn from details in the story and add it with what you already know.

Drawing a conclusion means to form an opinion. In order to do so, you use facts from what you read. You also use what you already know.

CHAPTER 6 REVIEW

ELA4R1g Inf

Read each passage and answer the questions that follow.

> The angry mother looked around her. What a mess! Her children had been very naughty. There was flour everywhere, broken eggs, and spilled milk. They had been trying to make cookies. Instead, they had made a mess. This simply would not do. She called out to her children, "Oh, boys…"

1. Which of the following seems MOST likely to happen next?

   A. The mother will hug her boys, and they will all have a food fight.

   B. The mother will scold her boys and make them clean up.

   C. The mother will tell her boys to go play while she naps.

   D. The mother will tell her boys to go nap while she cleans.

> A hungry lioness walks quietly through the tall grass. She has her prey in sight. At the edge of the water, a young impala drinks nervously. After pausing for a moment to listen, he continues lapping from the water. It is so hot, and he is so thirsty. The lioness draws closer and closer, careful not to disturb the grass too much. She is almost there. Suddenly…

2. Which of the following seems MOST likely to happen next?

   A. The lioness will decide that she is not hungry and let the impala go.

   B. The impala will turn and try to attack the lioness, and the lioness will run away.

   C. The lioness will try to attack the impala while the impala tries to escape.

   D. The lioness will go to the water and take a drink with the impala.

> Andy and Lorraine sit on the back porch and drink lemonade. Sweating, they fan away flies and watch the blowing leaves of the tree in the yard. Listening for the sound of the ice cream truck, they daydream about what they will buy.

3. Based upon the passage, which of the following is MOST likely true?
   A. It is a hot summer day.   C. It is a chilly autumn day.

   B. It is a cold winter day.   D. It is a rainy spring day.

> Gilbert stood outside of the candy store and looked in the window. He looked at the money in his hands and the rock candy sticks in the big jar on Mr. Kim's counter. There were so many colors, so many shapes. All he wanted was one of them. Gilbert counted the money over and over again. Finally, he sighed and started to walk home.

4. Based upon the passage, which of the following is MOST likely true?
   A. Gilbert has lots of rock candy at home.

   B. Gilbert has the money to buy the candy but decides not to.

   C. Gilbert does not like Mr. Kim or Mr. Kim's store.

   D. Gilbert doesn't have enough money to buy the candy.

> The Carters had spent most of Friday afternoon cleaning the house. They had vacuumed the floors, changed sheets, scrubbed tubs, and even washed windows. Every pillow was fluffed, and every speck of dust was gone. Although they were tired, they knew it had to be done.

5. Based upon the passage, which of the following is MOST likely true?
   A. The Carter family does spring cleaning every week.

   B. The Carter family is expecting an important guest.

   C. The Carter family hardly ever cleans the house.

   D. The Carter family is allergic to dirt and dust.

Mercedes was very excited. Today was her birthday. There would be a party with cake and ice cream. There would be family and friends gathered in the backyard. They would have a cookout, and there would be music, games, and dancing. She couldn't wait to get home. As she thought about the party ahead, she didn't even notice how hot it was today, or how her feet were starting to  hurt from walking so quickly in her school shoes. Finally, Mercedes was at home. She burst through the door, expecting to see decorations and party favors. As Mercedes looked around and announced her arrival, she was disappointed by what she saw. Her heart sank.

6. Based upon the passage, which of the following is MOST likely true?

   A. Mercedes doesn't see any party favors or decorations.

   B. Mercedes sees a room full of smiling family and friends.

   C. Mercedes sees a room full of party decorations.

   D. Mercedes doesn't see her mother in the living room.

Anthony and Bobby stood in a long line for the popular new roller coaster ride. Anthony nervously shoved his hand in the pocket of his jacket. While it wasn't very chilly out, Anthony was pretty nervous. He had heard that this ride was really scary. Without letting Bobby see, Anthony cut his eyes to sneak quick glances at the brave  people that were exiting the ride. Some of them looked relieved. Others looked scared. A few looked like they had just had the thrill of their lives. As the line moved, Anthony grew more and more nervous. Glancing behind him, he wondered about a way to get out of this.

7. Which of the following seems MOST likely to happen next?

   A. Anthony will decide that he is no longer afraid to ride the roller coaster.

   B. Anthony will ask someone whether or not he should ride the roller coaster.

   C. Anthony will make an excuse and get out of the line for the roller coaster.

   D. none of these

What a day! It had started with Adil tipping over the class ant farm. Keisha had knocked over Mrs. Wilson's pink coffee cup all over yesterday's math test. To make matters worse, after a wild recess, Mrs. Wilson's neat gray skirt was filthy with mud and grass stains. Now, it was quiet reading time, and Mrs. Wilson sat at her desk trying to read the answers on the coffee-stained math papers. Suddenly, there was a noise from the back of the room. Glancing up from the papers, Mrs. Wilson sees possibly the biggest disturbance of the day.

8. Which of the following seems MOST likely to happen next?

   A. Mrs. Wilson realizes that students are asleep in the back of the room.

   B. Mrs. Wilson realizes that all the hamsters are out of their cage.

   C. Mrs. Wilson realizes that the school principal is sitting quietly in the back.

   D. Mrs. Wilson realizes that all of her students are reading quietly.

Chapter 7
Graphics

This chapter addresses the following GPS-based CRCT standard(s):

ELA4R1 The student demonstrates comprehension and shows evidence of a warranted and responsible explanation of a variety of literary and informational texts.

For **informational texts**, the student reads and comprehends in order to develop understanding and expertise and produces evidence of reading that:

c. Identifies and uses knowledge of common graphic features (e.g., charts, maps, diagrams, illustrations).

How do you work your new handheld game? How do you assemble your new scooter? Could you tell a friend how to get to your house? Reading is a good way to learn something new. However, sometimes a picture is even better. **Graphics** are pictures that show information. A picture that shows how to assemble a scooter is a graphic. A map to your house is a graphic. Charts and graphs are other kinds of graphics.

DIAGRAMS

A **diagram** is a picture that shows the parts of something. A diagram can also show how something works. Below is a diagram of our solar system.

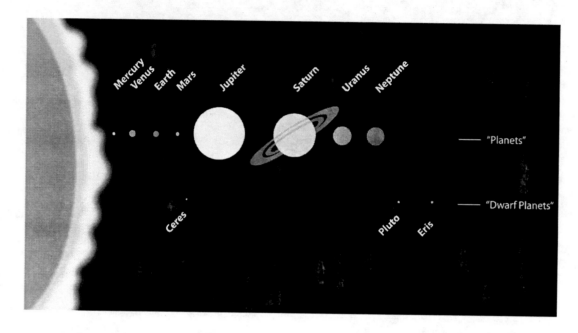

Did you notice that the diagram has both a picture and words? The words and the picture work together to explain the solar system.

See if you can answer the following questions by looking at the diagram of the solar system.

- Which planet is closest to the sun? (Mercury)
- Which planet is between Mars and Saturn? (Jupiter)
- Name one of the dwarf planets. (Ceres, Pluto, or Eris)

Practice 1: Diagrams

ELA4R1c Inf

Look at the diagram of the ladybug. Then, answer the questions that follow.

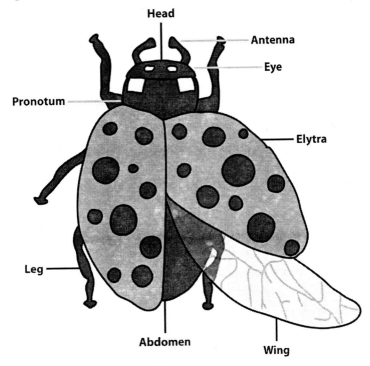

1. How many eyes does a ladybug have?

    A. two   B. four   C. six   D. eight

2. What is the name of the spotted part of the shell?

    A. wing   C. abdomen

    B. elytra   D. leg

3. Where is the wing?

    A. on the head   C. under the pronotum

    B. under the elytra   D. behind the fourth pair of legs

4. Which part connects to the head?

    A. leg   C. abdomen

    B. wing   D. antenna

ILLUSTRATIONS

An **illustration** is a picture. These pictures work with words. They make words easier to understand. They can be drawings or photographs.

For example, a science book can describe a stalactite. If there is also a photo, a stalactite is easier to understand. Here's how it works:

Having a picture to go with the words makes it easier to understand what a stalactite looks like.

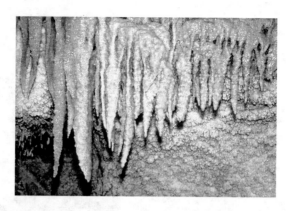

A stalactite hangs in a cave. It is made by water dripping very slowly for a long time. The water has minerals in it. As it hardens, it makes a stalactite.

Practice 2: Illustrations

ELA4R1c Inf

Look at this illustration of clouds. Then, answer the questions that follow.

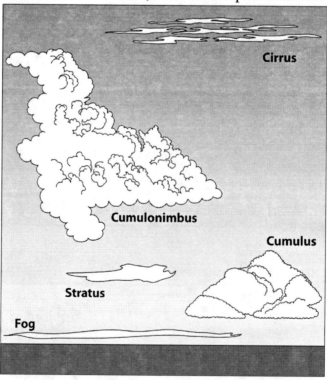

1. Which cloud looks like a single streak?

    A. fog

    B. stratus

    C. cumulus

    D. cumulonimbus

2. Which cloud is tallest?

    A. fog

    B. cumulus

    C. cumulonimbus

    D. cirrus

3. Which cloud is highest in the sky?

    A. cumulonimbus

    B. fog

    C. stratus

    D. cirrus

4. Which cloud looks like a group of thin streaks?

    A. fog

    B. cumulus

    C. cumulonimbus

    D. cirrus

CHARTS

A **chart** shows information using a picture. A chart is a quick way to see how things are related.

Read the paragraph below.

> My fourth grade class voted on its favorite ice cream flavors. Chocolate and vanilla tied for first place. Each flavor got seven votes. Strawberry came in second with four votes. Cookies and cream was the least popular. It got just two votes.

Now, look at the **bar graph** below. All of the facts from the paragraph above are in the chart.

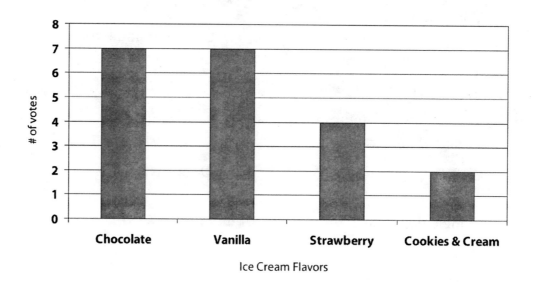

Class Poll
Favorite Ice Cream Flavors

A chart can make information easier to see than words can. The ice cream chart gives a quick picture of this class's ice cream preferences.

Another common kind of chart is a **pie chart**. A pie chart looks like this:

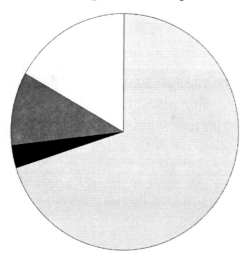

Pie charts show parts of the whole. On this pie chart, you can see that the lightest gray takes up more space than any other color. Which color takes up the least space?

If you said black, you're right!

Practice 3: Charts

ELA4R1c Inf

Read the chart below. Then, answer the questions that follow.

Class Poll
Favorite Authors

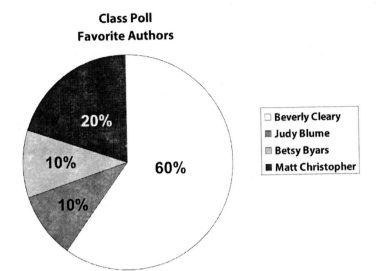

☐ Beverly Cleary
▨ Judy Blume
▨ Betsy Byars
■ Matt Christopher

1. What does this pie chart show?

   A. how many books the class has read

   B. the class's favorite authors

   C. who bought books at the book fair

   D. the most popular book in the class

2. Which author is the most popular?
   A. Judy Blume   C. Beverly Cleary

   B. Matt Christopher   D. Betsy Byars

3. What percent of the vote did Matt Christopher get?
   A. 60%   B. 20%   C. 10%   D. 100%

4. Which two authors got an equal number of votes?

   A. Betsy Byars and Matt Christopher

   B. Judy Blume and Matt Christopher

   C. Betsy Byars and Beverly Cleary

   D. Judy Blume and Betsy Byars

MAPS

Maps are graphics that show places. Maps can show a large place, like the world. Maps can show smaller places, like the town you live in. Some maps show streets. Some maps show rivers and mountains.

Now look at the next map.

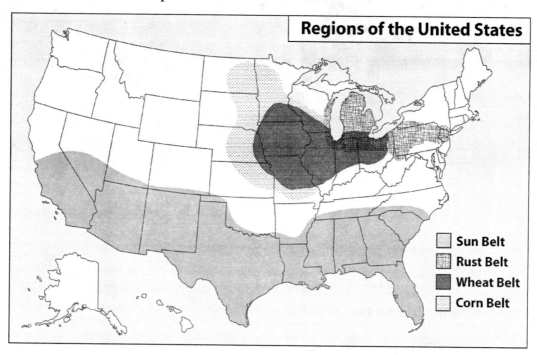

Most maps have a title to tell you what you are looking at. The title of this map is "Regions of the United States."

Some maps also have a **legend**. A legend tells what symbols on the map mean.

The legend in the map above tells what the colors mean. By reading the legend, you can see which regions of the country are known by which names.

For example, by looking at the legend, you can tell that the southern part of the United States is called the Sun Belt. That section is gray on the map, which matches the gray part of the legend that says Sun Belt.

Practice 4: Maps

ELA4R1c Inf

Look at the map below. Then, answer the questions that follow.

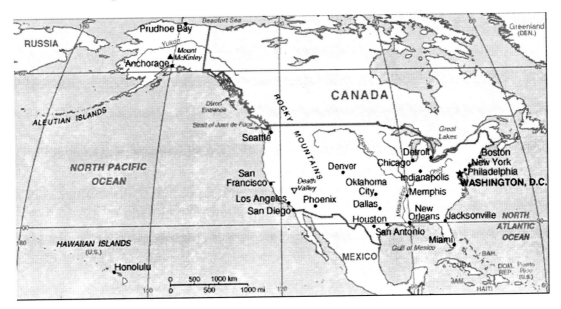

1. What does the map mostly show?

    A. the United States

    B. African rivers

    C. Canadian provinces

    D. roads

2. Which country shares a border with the United States?
    A. Cuba   B. Mexico   C. Hawaii   D. Russia

3. Which mountain range runs through Canada and the United States?
    A. the Alps

    B. the Rocky Mountains

    C. the Missouri

    D. the Apennines

4. Which ocean is closest to the city of San Francisco?
    A. the Gulf of Mexico

    B. the Hawaiian Islands

    C. the North Pacific Ocean

    D. the North Atlantic Ocean

CHAPTER 7 SUMMARY

Graphics are sometimes used along with words. They are pictures that help people understand the words. There are different types of graphics.

- A **diagram** is a drawing that explains how something works or shows the parts of something. A bicycle helmet comes with a diagram. The diagram shows how the helmet should fit.

- An **illustration** is a picture a writer uses to make something easier to understand. A photograph of an author is one kind of illustration.

- A **chart** shows information using a picture. A pie chart is one kind of chart.

- A **map** shows place. A road map is one kind of map.

CHAPTER 7 REVIEW

ELA4R1c Inf

Read the information, and answer the questions.

Pretend that you just got a new bicycle. The last step of assembling it is to put on the reflectors. Look at the diagram. Then, answer the questions that follow.

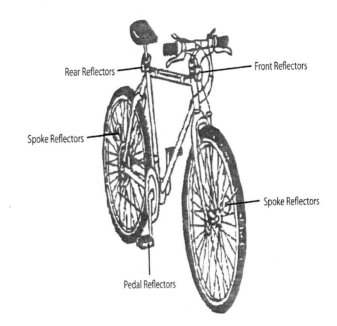

1. Where should you put the rear reflector?

    A. on the pedal

    B. on the handlebars

    C. on the front spokes

    D. below the seat

2. How many front reflectors are there?
    A. one   B. two   C. three   D. four

3. Where do the spoke reflectors go?
    A. on the pedals and the handlebars   C. on the seat and the wheels

    B. on the front and back wheels   D. on the seat and the rear wheel

Look at the illustrations below. Then, answer the questions that follow.

| 1 | 2 | 3 | 4 |

4. Which picture is the BEST illustration to go with this sentence?

"Even as a boy, Albert Einstein showed unusual intelligence."

A. picture 1   B. picture 2   C. picture 3   D. picture 4

5. Which picture is the BEST illustration to go with this sentence?

"People still like to visit the house where Einstein once lived."

A. picture 1   B. picture 2   C. picture 3   D. picture 4

Read the chart below. Then, answer the questions that follow.

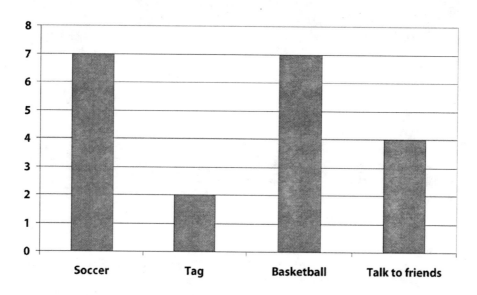

Favorite Recess Activities

6. Which four activities are shown on the graph?

A. talk to friends, skip rope, soccer, basketball

B. eat a snack, tag, soccer, talk to friends

C. talk to friends, tag, basketball, soccer

D. soccer, basketball, baseball, football

7. Which two activities got the same number of votes?

A. tag and basketball   C. talk with friends and tag

B. soccer and basketball   D. tag and soccer

8. How many people voted for the least popular activity?
   A. 1   B. 2   C. 3   D. 4

Look at the map below. Then, answer the questions that follow.

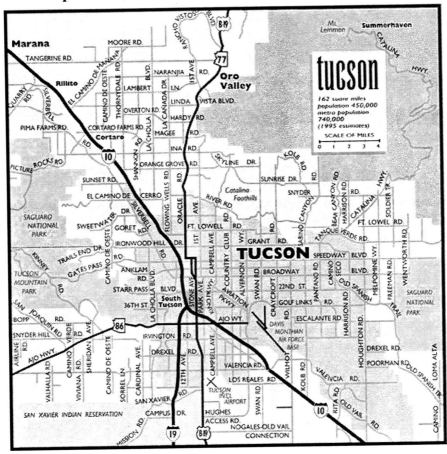

9. What area does this map show?

   A. Tucson   C. the Atlantic Ocean

   B. Washington, D.C.   D. New York City

10. Which highway runs through the San Xavier Indian Reservation on this map?
    A. 10   B. 19   C. 86   D. 21

Chapter 8
Reading Literature

This chapter addresses the following GPS-based CRCT standard(s):

> **ELA4R1** The student demonstrates comprehension and shows evidence of a warranted and responsible explanation of a variety of literary and informational texts.
>
> For **literary texts**, the student identifies the characteristics of various genres and produces evidence of reading that:
>
> **b.** Identifies and analyzes the elements of plot, character, and setting in stories read, written, viewed, or performed.
>
> **c.** Identifies the speaker of a poem or story.
>
> **e.** Identifies and shows the relevance of foreshadowing clues.
>
> **f.** Makes judgments and inferences about setting, characters, and events and supports them with elaborating and convincing evidence from the text.

You may not realize it, but you have read quite a bit of literature in your life. In school, and maybe on your own too, you have read stories, books, poems, and maybe even plays. It's time to learn a little more about the kinds of literature you are reading.

TYPES OF LITERATURE

Which do you like best—short stories, plays, or poems? All three are types of **literature**. Literature is writing that uses imagination. There are many different kinds of literature. Read on to see which kinds you already know.

Types of Literature

Drama is literature that is acted out. A play like *Peter Pan* is an example of drama.

A **fable** is a short story that teaches a lesson. Fables often use animals in place of humans. "The Tortoise and the Hare" is a fable that teaches the lesson, "slow and steady wins the race."

Folktales are stories that are passed down over many years. They usually begin, "Once upon a time…" *Cinderella* is an example of a folktale.

A **legend** is a story that has some true and some untrue parts. Legends are usually about people. Stories about Robin Hood make up a legend. Robin Hood may have been a real person, but no one is sure exactly who he was or what he did.

A **narrative** is a story. Any type of literature can be a narrative. The Ramona books by Beverly Cleary are narratives.

A **poem** is a writing filled with emotion. Poems do not need to have full sentences or punctuation like other writing. A poem may or may not rhyme. An example of a poem is "Hey Diddle Diddle."

A **short story** is shorter than a chapter book. "Rip Van Winkle" is a short story.

Practice 1: Types of Literature

ELA4R1 Lit

Answer the questions that follow.

1. This fall, my class acted out the story of the first Thanksgiving. This is an example of a
   A. poem.   B. drama.   C. fable.   D. short story.

2. My sister is memorizing some common nursery rhymes. She is working on "Three Blind Mice" and "Humpty Dumpty." Both are examples of

   A. poems.

   B. legends.

   C. dramas.

   D. folktales.

3. "The Boy Who Cried Wolf" teaches us that if you lie, people won't believe you when you do tell the truth. This is an example of a
   A. poem.   B. drama.   C. fable.   D. legend.

4. "Rumpelstiltskin" is a story that has been told for many years. This is an example of
   A. drama.   B. folktale.   C. fable.   D. short story.

ELEMENTS OF LITERATURE

A story has many parts. A writer uses people, places, and ideas to tell a story. These are called the **elements of literature**. Elements are parts like plot, setting, and characters. Read on to learn about the elements of literature.

PLOT

Plot is what happens in a story. If you were telling the plot of "Jack and the Beanstalk," you might say, "Jack trades his cow for some magic beans. He plants the beans, and a tall beanstalk grows up to the sky. Jack climbs it and steals from a giant. The giant chases Jack, but Jack gets away."

An author usually tells us the plot in the order that it happens. Sometimes the writer might mix up the order to make the story more interesting.

FORESHADOWING

Sometimes a writer gives us a clue about something that is going to happen in the plot. This is called **foreshadowing**.

Read this example of foreshadowing.

In the American Girl book *Changes for Molly*, Molly gets to be the star in a dance production. The author spends part of the book telling how much Molly wants to be the star. We read how excited she is and how hard she practices. Just before the big night, Molly mentions that her throat hurts. When we read this, we have a hint that she may be getting sick. If Molly were sick, she could not be in the show. Because of the foreshadowing, we are not surprised to read, later in the story, that Molly starts to feel worse. She has to miss the big show. Foreshadowing gets the reader ready for what will happen.

In addition to what the author says, you also can figure out some things on your own.

SETTING

Setting is where and when a story takes place. The setting of a story could be Georgia during the Civil War. The setting of a play could be Mars in the year 2250. A writer uses setting to help tell a story.

Read the passage below.

> Everywhere I looked was whirling snow. Though it was around noon, the sky looked gray through the blizzard. I knew my house was not far away, but I couldn't tell which way to go in the fierce storm.

The setting in the passage above is midday in a winter blizzard. We can tell that the story takes place somewhere that has a winter full of snow. The setting makes us wonder how the person will get home. We can predict that the speaker will have a hard journey.

MAKING INFERENCES ABOUT LITERATURE

As you read, foreshadowing is one way you can figure out what will happen in a story. Another way is to infer. **Inferences** are guesses. To infer, you use what the author tells you to figure out other things. Your guess might make a judgment about a character. Or, you might guess how the plot will turn out. When you guess, you use what you know to figure something out.

Read the next passage.

John is late to school every day. He leaves his house on time each morning to catch the bus. But, he always has to go back inside. Some mornings, he goes back for his lunch. Other mornings, it is to get his homework. One morning he even left without his shoes!

From the passage, you can infer that John is forgetful. The author did not say, "John is forgetful," but you can guess that he is from the information you do know.

Now, predict what will happen when John goes on a camping trip. If you inferred that he will forget something, you are right!

CHARACTERS

Characters are the people (or animals) in the story. Characters help tell a story. Henry Huggins is a character in *Henry and Ribsy*. He is the main character because the story is mostly about him. His dog, Ribsy, is a character in the story too.

Writers tell us things about the characters so we can get to know them. On the next page are some ways writers tell us about the people in a story.

Getting to Know a Character		
Looks	**Actions**	**Words**
Are his or her clothes fancy or ragged?	Is the character kind to others?	Is the character smart?
Does he have a scar?	Does he start fights?	Does he speak with an accent?
What color is her hair?	How does she start her day?	Is she afraid to say what she thinks?

You can learn about the characters in a story by paying attention. What does the writer tell you about them? How do they talk? What do they do? You can also infer things about characters, just like you can about plot and setting. Here is an example.

- If a character wears rags, you can guess he might be poor.
- If a character speaks with an accent, you can guess that she comes from far away.

Practice 2: Elements of Literature

ELA4R1b, e, f Lit

Read the passages. Then, answer the questions.

In this book, a boy moves to a new town. At first, it is hard to make new friends. The main character likes to be by himself and work on his computer. Then, he meets a friend who likes computers too. The boy ends up being glad he moved.

1. The above is an example of

    A. plot.

    B. setting.

    C. characters.

    D. foreshadowing.

> "I am a brave person. There is only one thing that scares me—spiders! I sure hope I don't meet any spiders when I go down into the basement."

2. What do you predict will be in the basement?
   A. flies   B. ghosts   C. spiders   D. buckets

> "Say, Jan, this isn't any fun!"
>
> "What do you want to play then, Ted?"
>
> Janet Martin looked at her brother, who was dressed in one of his father's coats and hats while across his nose was a pair of spectacles much too large for him. Janet, wearing one of her mother's skirts, was sitting in a chair holding a doll.
>
> – from *The Curlytops at Uncle Frank's Ranch* by Howard R. Garis

3. What are the children doing?
   A. playing a game of baseball   C. riding in the family car

   B. studying spelling words   D. playing a game of pretend

4. The game was MOST likely whose idea?
   A. Jan's idea   C. their father's idea

   B. Ted's idea   D. Uncle Frank's idea

5. What will happen next?
   A. They will keep playing the game.

   B. They will stop playing the game.

   C. They will start singing.

   D. They will bake a cake.

The Bobbsey family lived in the large town of Lakeport, situated at the head of Lake Metoka, a clear and beautiful sheet of water upon which the twins loved to go boating. Mr. Richard Bobbsey was a lumber merchant, with a large yard and docks on the lake shore, and a saw and planning mill close by. The house was a quarter of a mile away, on a fashionable street and had a small but nice garden around it, and a barn in the rear, in which the children loved at times to play.

– from *The Bobbsey Twins* by Laura Lee Hope

6. What is the setting?
    A. the Bobbsey kitchen

    B. the lumber mill

    C. the back yard

    D. the town of Lakeport

7. What do you predict this book will mostly be about?
    A. the Bobbsey children

    B. the town of Lakeport

    C. the Bobbseys' barn

    D. boating on the lake

Bunny Brown was a great one for asking questions. So was his sister Sue; but Sue would often wait a while and find things out for herself, instead of asking strangers what certain things meant. Bunny always seemed in a hurry, and his mother used to say he could ask more questions than several grown folks could answer.

– from *Bunny Brown and His Sister Sue* by Laura Lee Hope

8. Which of the following BEST describes Bunny Brown?
    A. He thinks about things on his own.

    B. He helps his sister figure things out.

    C. He likes to ask questions.

    D. He waits before he talks.

9. Which of the following words BEST describes Sue?

   A. patient   B. nosy   C. unfriendly   D. loud

10. Who is MOST likely to have adventures?

   A. Sue   C. their mother

   B. Bunny Brown   D. the strangers

POINT OF VIEW

Pretend that you are on the playground. Two boys are arguing over who had a ball first. Ask each boy what happened, and you will get two different stories. Each boy has his own point of view. **Point of view** is how a person sees the world. A story will differ depending on who is telling it.

In literature, the person who tells the story is the **narrator**. The narrator's point of view depends on who he or she is. Think about the story of the "Three Little Pigs." If the pigs told the story, what would they say? If the wolf told the story, how would the story be different?

A writer chooses who tells a story. There are two main points of view.

First person	Third person
The narrator is one of the characters.	The narrator may or may not be in the story. He or she may or may not know what the characters are thinking.
The narrator uses *I* to tell the story.	The narrator uses *he*, *she*, and *they* to tell the story.

Practice 3: Point of View

ELA4R1c Lit

Answer the following questions.

1. Which sentence is in the first person point of view?

    A. For summer vacation, the Kellers went to the beach.

    B. Peter and his brother Fudge lived in New York.

    C. I don't think it's fair being the youngest in the family.

    D. Jessie was the most daring of the children.

2. Which sentence is in the third person point of view?

    A. I wish I had a pet giraffe.

    B. My friend and I like to play hockey.

    C. When I was in first grade, I was shy.

    D. Mrs. Miller has the largest class.

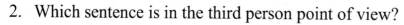

"My little sister Elsa is so annoying! She tags along after me and bothers me when I play with my friends," said Juan.

3. What might Elsa's point of view be?

    A. Juan is right. I am an annoying sister.

    B. Juan is such a kind brother.

    C. Juan is mean and won't let me play.

    D. Juan always lets me play, too.

Dogs are the best pets in the world! They are much better than cats or fish.

4. Who likely said this?

A. a person who likes dogs

B. a person who likes cats

C. a person who likes fish

D. a person who has no pets

CHAPTER 8 SUMMARY

In this chapter, you learned about literature. There are different **types of literature**. Some types of literature are **drama**, **fable**, **folk tale**, **legend**, **narrative**, **poem**, and **short story**.

Writers use **elements of literature** to tell their stories.

- **Plot** is what happens in the story.
- **Setting** is where and when the story happens.
- **Characters** are the people or animals that a story is about.
- **Point of view** is how a person sees the world. A story will change based on who is telling it.

Writers help us figure things out about the story and the people in it.

- With **foreshadowing**, a writer gives us a hint about something that will happen later.
- When we **make inferences**, we guess based on what we know.

CHAPTER 8 REVIEW

ELA4R1b, c, e, f Lit

Read the passages below. Then, answer the questions.

1. Which term means what happens in a story?

    A. foreshadowing   C. setting

    B. plot   D. characters

2. Which terms means giving clues about what is going to happen?

    A. foreshadowing   C. setting

    B. plot   D. characters

3. Pretend you got a postcard from a friend. Unscramble the sentences to put the events in order.

    1 On Tuesday, we swam in a lagoon.

    2 We are having fun on our cruise.

    3 On Monday, we snorkeled with sharks.

    4 This has been the best trip ever. I wish you were here!

    5 By Wednesday, we were ready to stay on the ship and rest!

    A. 1, 2, 3, 4, 5   C. 3, 2, 4, 5, 1

    B. 5, 4, 3, 2, 1   D. 2, 3, 1, 5, 4

4. What kind of literature is the writing on the post card?

    A. a drama   C. a narrative

    B. a poem   D. a folktale

> Happy Jack Squirrel had had a wonderful day. He had found some big chestnut-trees that he had never seen before, and which promised to give him all the nuts he would want for all the next winter. Now he was thinking of going home, for it was getting late in the afternoon. He looked out across the open field where Mr. Goshawk had nearly caught him that morning. His home was on the other side.
>
> "It's a long way 'round," said Happy Jack to himself, "but it is best to be safe and sure."
>
> – from "Happy Jack Squirrel Makes a Find" by Thornton W. Burgess

5. What can you infer about Happy Jack Squirrel when he says, "it is best to be safe and sure"?

    A. He is careful.

    B. He is daring.

    C. He is a baby.

    D. He is fast.

6. What point of view does the author use?

    A. first person

    B. second person

    C. third person

    D. fourth person

7. What will MOST likely happen next in the story?

    A. He will be rewarded for his caution.

    B. He will get lost on the way home.

    C. He will be crowned king.

    D. He will lose everything he has worked for.

> It was just on the edge of the twilight. The little Peppers, (except Ben, the oldest) were enjoying a "breathing spell," as their mother called it. This meant some quiet work suitable for the hour. This was all the "breathing spell" they could remember, poor things. Times were always hard with them nowadays. Father had died when Phronsie was a baby. Mrs. Pepper had had hard work to scrape together money enough to put bread into her children's mouths, and to pay the rent of the little brown house.
>
> – adapted from *Five Little Peppers and How They Grew*
> by Margaret Sidney

8. What can you tell about the Peppers?
   A. They are rich.
   B. They are poor.
   C. They are sick.
   D. They are lazy.

9. What is the setting?
   A. a castle at dawn
   B. a boat lost in the ocean
   C. Mars in the morning
   D. the Pepper home at twilight

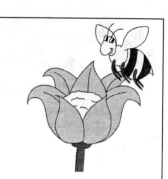

Burly, dozing humble-bee,

Where thou art is clime for me.

Let them sail for Porto Rique,

Far-off heats through seas to seek;

I will follow thee alone,

Thou animated torrid-zone!

– from "The Humble-Bee" by Ralph Waldo Emerson

10. What type of literature is this?
    A. a narrative
    B. a legend
    C. a poem
    D. a short story

11. What point of view does the author use?
    A. first person
    B. second person
    C. third person
    D. fourth person

12. What can you tell about the narrator?
    A. He is afraid of insects.
    B. He does not like hot weather.
    C. He wants to sail the seas.
    D. He likes bees.

Chapter 9
Literary Devices

This chapter addresses the following GPS-based CRCT standard(s):

ELA4R1 The student demonstrates comprehension and shows evidence of a warranted responsible explanation of a variety of literary and informational texts.

For **literary texts**, the student identifies the characteristics of various genres and produces evidence of reading that:

d. Identifies sensory details and figurative language.

i. Identifies rhyme and rhythm, repetition, similes, and sensory images in poems.

Have you ever heard the saying, "Choose your words carefully"? Words are important to writers. Writers choose their words carefully. Writers think about how their writing sounds. Writers have different ways to make words come alive.

FIGURATIVE LANGUAGE

In chapter 8, you learned about literature. You learned how writers show imagination with words. Writers choose words with extra meaning. This is called **figurative language**. Authors write this way when they want a reader to see something a certain way. Read on to learn about some types of figurative language.

Figurative Language

Imagery	Imagery is writing that appeals to the five senses. The words describe how things feel, taste, sound, look, and smell.	**Example:** Icy fingers of air crept under the curtain. It billowed like the cape of a flying superhero.
Metaphor	A metaphor compares things directly, without using *like* or *as*.	**Example:** His smile was a ray of sunshine.
Personification	Personification means to give human qualities to something which is not human.	**Example:** The sun smiled down on us cheerfully.
Simile	A simile compares two unlike things using *like* or *as*.	**Example:** He is as happy as a puppy with a new chew toy.

Practice 1: Figurative Language

ELA4R1d, i Lit

Read the passages. Then, answer the questions that follow.

> The comet walks a path through the sky at night. It shines as bright as a spotlight. It is a guide through the dark. Follow the comet with me.

1. Which of the following is a simile?

    A. The comet walks a path through the sky at night.

    B. It shines as bright as a spotlight.

    C. The comet is a guide through the dark.

    D. Follow the comet with me.

2. Which of the following is a metaphor?

A. The comet walks a path through the sky at night.

B. It shines as bright as a spotlight.

C. The comet is a guide through the dark.

D. Follow the comet with me.

3. Which of the following shows personification?

A. The comet walks a path through the sky at night.

B. It shines as bright as a spotlight.

C. The comet is a guide through the dark.

D. Follow the comet with me.

> The moon has a face like the clock in the hall;
> She shines on thieves on the garden wall,
> On streets and field and harbour quays,
> And birdies asleep in the forks of the trees.
> The squalling cat and the squeaking mouse,
> The howling dog by the door of the house,
> The bat that lies in bed at noon,
> All love to be out by the light of the moon.
>
> – from "The Moon" by Robert Louis Stevenson

4. "The moon has a face like the clock in the hall," is an example of

  A. a simile.   C. something to hear.

  B. a metaphor.   D. something to touch.

5. "The squalling cat and the squeaking mouse, / The howling dog by the door of the house" appeals to which of the five senses?

  A. touch   B. hearing   C. taste   D. smell

POETRY

In chapter 8, you learned that **poetry** is one type of literature. Writers often use poetry to show feelings. Now, we'll talk more about what makes poems special.

Sound is important in poetry. Poetry is meant to be spoken aloud. When you read a poem, try reading it out loud. Listen to how the poem sounds. Some poems are even set to music.

Here are some ways poets use sound:

RHYME

When the ending sounds of words are the same, they **rhyme**. Sometimes, poets use rhyme in their poems. Rhyme carries a poem along. It adds movement to the poem. Not all poems rhyme.

The poem below does rhyme. The words in bold show the rhyme.

Rock-a-bye, baby
In the **treetop**
When the wind blows
The cradle will **rock**
When the bough breaks
The cradle will **fall**
And down will come baby
Cradle and **all**

– from "Rock-a-bye, Baby" author unknown

RHYTHM

Poets also use rhythm to make a poem sound a certain way. **Rhythm** is the pattern of stressed and unstressed syllables. When you read a poem aloud, the rhythm is the up and down sound your voice makes. Rhythm makes the poem feel like it is moving.

A limerick is a poem that has a particular rhythm. Read the limerick below aloud. Listen for the rhythm.

> There once was a man from Kew
>
> Who found a dead mouse in his stew.
>
> Said the waiter, "Don't shout
>
> Or wave it about,
>
> Or the rest will be wanting one too!"

Did you hear how your voice went up and down? That pattern of up and down is the poem's rhythm. It's almost like reading a song.

REPETITION

Another way poets use sound is through repetition. **Repetition** is using a certain sound more than once. This brings attention to certain words. Repetition also adds to the rhythm of a poem.

Rhyme is one way a poet can use repetition. Remember, rhyme repeats the end sounds of words. Here are three other types of repetition:

Alliteration: the repetition of similar sounds at the beginning of words

A tongue twister uses alliteration.

> **Example:** "She sells seashells by the seashore."

Assonance: the repetition of similar vowel sounds

> **Example:** In "Twinkle, twinkle little star," the short *i* sound is repeated in the first line.

Consonance: the repetition of similar consonant sounds

> **Example:** This line from Robert Frost's "Stopping by Woods on a Snowy Evening" repeats the *w* sound: "To watch his woods fill up with snow."

Practice 2: Poetry

ELA4R1i Lit

Read the poems below. Then, answer the questions.

---

1 How do you like to go up in a swing,

2 Up in the air so blue?

3 Oh, I do think it the pleasantest thing

4 Ever a child can do!

5 Up in the air and over the wall,

6 Till I can see so wide,

7 Rivers and trees and cattle and all

8 Over the countryside—

9 Till I look down on the garden green,

10 Down on the roof so brown—

11 Up in the air I go flying again,

12 Up in the air and down!

– "The Swing" by Robert Louis Stevenson

---

1. Line 5 ends with *wall*. Which line rhymes with line 5?

    A. line 6, *wide*

    B. line 7, *all*

    C. line 8, *countryside*

    D. line 9, *green*

2. The repetition in line 10, "Down on the roof so brown," is an example of
    A. imagery.   B. metaphor.   C. simile.   D. assonance.

3. What movement does the poet MOST likely intend you to think of in this poem?

    A. jogging through the quiet forest

    B. moving back and forth in the swing

    C. playing scales on the piano

    D. sweeping the floor with a broom

4. Why do you think the poet repeats the word *up* so often in this poem?

    A. to be like the repeated motion of the swing

    B. because he couldn't think of any other words

    C. because he likes the word *up*

    D. he wanted all of the lines to start with *up*

> Peter Piper picked a peck of pickled peppers.
> Did Peter Piper pick a peck of pickled peppers?

5. What sound is repeated in these two lines?

    A. *a*

    B. *r*

    C. *p*

    D. *s*

6. This is an example of

    A. simile.

    B. personification.

    C. alliteration.

    D. metaphor.

CHAPTER 9 SUMMARY

In this chapter, you learned about ways writers use words.

Writers use **figurative language** to be imaginative. Some of the kinds of figurative language are:

- **Personification**: to give human qualities to something that is not human
- **Simile**: to compare using *like* or *as*
- **Metaphor**: to compare directly, without using *like* or *as*
- **Imagery**: writing that appeals to the five senses

Poetry is a type of literature that shows feelings. Poems are meant to be read aloud. Sound is important to poets. Sound helps to show movement in poetry.

Ways poets use sound:

- **Rhyme**: the ending sounds of words are the same
- **Rhythm**: the pattern of stressed and unstressed syllables
- **Repetition**: using a sound more than once
- **Alliteration**: the repetition of similar sounds at the beginning of words
- **Assonance**: the repetition of similar vowel sounds
- **Consonance:** the repetition of similar consonant sounds

CHAPTER 9 REVIEW

ELA4R1d, i Lit

Read the passages. Then, answer the questions.

> Say, whose is the skill that paints valley and hill,
>
> Like a picture so fair to the sight?
>
> That flecks the green meadow with sunshine and shadow,
>
> Till the little lambs leap with delight?
>
> 'Tis a secret untold to hearts cruel and cold,
>
> Though 'tis sung by the angels above,
>
> In notes that ring clear for the ears that can hear—
>
> And the name of the secret is Love!
>
> For I think it is Love,
>
> For I feel it is Love,
>
> For I'm sure it is nothing but Love!
>
> – from "A Song of Love" by Lewis Carroll

1. What sound is repeated in this line?

   Say, whose is the skill that paints valley and hill,

   A. *e*   B. *l*   C. *p*   D. *o*

2. This repetition is an example of
   A. rhyme.   B. rhythm.   C. assonance.   D. consonance.

3. Love painting the valleys and hills is an example of what kind of figurative language?
   A. alliteration   C. metaphor

   B. personification   D. simile

> 1 The sun is not a-bed, when I
>
> 2 At night upon my pillow lie;
>
> 3 Still round the earth his way he takes,
>
> 4 And morning after morning makes.
>
> – from "The Sun Travels" by Robert Louis Stevenson

4. In line 3, "Still round the earth his way he takes," what is the poet talking about?

    A. the pillow   B. the night   C. the bed   D. the sun

5. What picture does the poet show of the sun's journey in this poem?

    A. a circular movement

    B. a back and forth pattern

    C. an up and down pattern

    D. a gliding movement

6. The last words in lines 3 and 4 of this poem sound the same. This is called

    A. alliteration.   B. rhythm.   C. rhyme.   D. simile.

7. Why does the poet likely repeat the word "morning" in line 4?

    A. He hopes to imitate the sun's journey.

    B. He likes the way it sounds.

    C. He hopes to make us go to sleep.

    D. He can't think of any other words.

> "Look at that cloud!" Cheng exclaimed. "It looks just like a pirate ship!"

8. In this line, Cheng used
   A. a metaphor.   B. a simile.   C. assonance.   D. rhyme.

> "I just can't think of the answer," Lauren wailed. "My mind is an empty box right now."

9. Lauren used
   A. a simile.   B. a metaphor.   C. alliteration.   D. rhythm.

> This little piggy went to market.
>
> This little piggy stayed home.

10. What sound is repeated in these lines?
    A. *s*   B. *p*   C. *m*   D. *i*

11. This repetition is an example of

    A. alliteration.

    B. rhythm.

    C. assonance.

    D. imagery.

> Hear the loud alarum bells—
>
> Brazen bells!
>
> What a tale of terror now their turbulency tells!
>
> – from "The Bells" by Edgar Allen Poe

12. Which two beginning sounds are repeated in these lines?

    A. *r* and *l*

    B. *b* and *t*

    C. *b* and *m*

    D. *h* and *w*

13. This repetition is an example of

    A. alliteration.

    B. assonance.

    C. simile.

    D. imagery.

14. The words at the end of each line are an example of

    A. personification.

    B. alliteration.

    C. metaphor.

    D. rhyme.

Chapter 10
Themes and Lessons in Literature

This chapter addresses the following GPS-based CRCT standard(s):

> **ELA4R1** The student demonstrates comprehension and shows evidence of a warranted and responsible explanation of a variety of literary and informational texts.
>
> For **literary texts**, the student identifies the characteristics of various genres and produces evidence of reading that:
>
> **h.** Identifies themes and lessons in folktales, tall tales, and fables.

Have you ever taken a phone message? The caller gives a short statement of what he wants to say. Writers can also give us messages. A writer can use a story to tell us his thoughts and ideas. Authors use many kinds of stories—especially folktales, tall tales, and fables—to give us messages in themes and lessons. Let's talk first about theme.

THEME

Theme is the message in a piece of literature. Themes point to things that people everywhere experience. For example, people living all over the world know what love is. One theme could be, "love is blind." Here are some other examples of themes:

Money can't buy happiness

You should always be honest.

Freedom is worth fighting for.

A writer does not come right out and tell us what the theme is. We need to find the theme by looking for clues. In chapter 8, you read about inferences. Inferences are guesses we make from things the author tells us. Looking at the plot and how the characters act can help us find the theme.

To find the theme, do the following:

- Look for clues in the title.
- Think about the story and how the author tells it.
- Write one sentence about what you think the author's message is.

Read the passage below. It is a tall tale, meaning that it is probably a story often about a real person but has some exaggeration. Use the steps above to find the theme.

The Legend of Johnny Appleseed

Johnny Appleseed lived over two hundred years ago, but he is still a legend today. Johnny spent his whole life planting apple trees and giving away apple seeds. He wanted everyone to have healthy food. He also wanted to see apple blossoms everywhere. Johnny's work helped feed the pioneers in the Midwest. He was known for his kindness to both people and animals. He was also very generous. Johnny chose a hard life to do what he believed in. He traveled on foot for thousands of miles. He put his wish to help others above his own comfort.

Look for clues in the title.

The title is "The Legend of Johnny Appleseed." Think about the things that make Johnny a legend.

Think about the story and how the author tells it.

What actions does the author tell about? Why does Johnny act as he does, and what happens as a result?

Write one sentence about what you think the author's message is.

What is the author trying to say about this man?

The writer told us what Johnny was like. We learned why Johnny acted as he did. We read about a generous man who put others ahead of himself. From this, we can see that the writer values Johnny's character. One theme of the passage could be the value of generosity and kindness.

Practice 1: Theme

ELA4R1h Lit

Read the passages below. Then, answer the questions.

The Fisherman and His Wife

Once there was a poor fisherman who lived with his wife in a hut by the sea. One day, the fisherman caught a fish that could speak.

"Please let me go," said the fish.

"I would not eat a fish that could talk!" said the fisherman. He let the fish go.

The fisherman went home and told his wife what had happened.

"You foolish man!" she shouted. "That was a magic fish. Go back, and ask him to change this hut into a cottage."

The fisherman did not want to go, but his wife made him. He went back to the sea, called the fish, and told him what he wanted.

"Go home," said the fish. "It is done."

The man went home and saw that his hut was now a nice cottage. His wife was happy but not for long. She wanted a bigger house. She made her husband go back to the fish and ask for a castle. Again, he did not want to go, but she made him.

He went back to the sea, called the fish, and told him what he wanted.

"Go home," said the fish. "It is done."

The man went home and saw that the cottage was now a castle. His wife was happy but not for long. Now, she wanted to be a queen. She made her husband go back to the fish and ask the fish to make her a queen. Again, he did not want to go, but she made him.

He went back to the sea, called the fish, and told him what he wanted.

"Go home," said the fish.

The man went home and saw that the castle was now his old hut. And there they live to this day.

— adapted from the folktale as told by the Brothers Grimm

---

1. What is the theme of this story?

   A. the joy of owning a house

   C. the importance of money

   B. the results of greed

   D. the sadness of death

2. How does the author show us this theme?

   A. He shows how the wife is never satisfied.

   B. He shows that bigger is always better.

   C. He describes how two wrongs do not make a right.

   D. He shows how a house will always have problems.

King Midas and the Golden Touch

Once there was a rich king named Midas. King Midas loved gold. He thought about gold all the time. The one other thing that he loved besides gold was his daughter. He counted the gold he had and wished for more. One day, while he was counting his gold, he looked up to see a stranger standing over him.

"You are a rich man, King Midas," said the stranger.

"Yes, but it is not enough," Midas replied. "I wish that everything I touched would turn to gold. Then, I would have enough."

"You shall have the golden touch in the morning," the stranger said.

In the morning, King Midas jumped out of bed. He touched a chair. It turned to gold. He touched the bed and a table, and they turned to gold. When he went to eat his breakfast, the food turned to gold.

"I don't see how I am supposed to eat!" Midas cried.

Just then, his daughter came into the room. When he reached out to hug her, Midas found that his dear daughter had become a statue of gold. Midas cried out. He wished for his daughter to be herself again. Then, he saw the stranger.

"Well, Midas, how do you like the golden touch?" the stranger asked.

"I am so unhappy," Midas said. "Gold is not everything. I love my daughter more."

"You are wiser than you were, Midas," the stranger said. "Take this water, and sprinkle it on all of the things you touched."

Midas did. The first thing he sprinkled was his daughter. Right away, his dear daughter stood before him, no longer a gold statue. Midas was very happy.

3. What is the theme of this story?

   A. Having gold is better than having food.

   B. Everyone should be a king.

   C. People are worth more than money.

   D. It is good to be generous.

4. What does Midas say that helps us see the theme?

   A. "Yes, but it is not enough."

   B. "I wish that everything I touched would turn to gold."

   C. "I don't see how I am supposed to eat!"

   D. "Gold is not everything. I love my daughter more."

LESSONS IN LITERATURE

You just read that a writer uses theme to tell us ideas about people and life. Sometimes, an author writes a story to teach us how to act. The **lesson** is how the writer wants us to act. A writer makes the lesson of the story clear and easy to find.

A **folktale** is a story passed on by word of mouth. It is often very old. Many people retell it in different ways. These stories sometimes convey a moral lesson. Folktales are often simple stories set in the past. They can have animal, human, or supernatural characters. Examples of folktales that have been around for a long time include the story of the three little pigs and the tale of the beauty and the beast.

A **fable** is another kind of story that teaches a lesson. A writer will often use animals to tell the story. These animals act and think as people do. By telling the story of how these animals think, speak, and act, the writer is telling us how we should think, speak, and act. The lesson in a fable teaches us the right thing to do.

Read the following fable.

The Lion and the Mouse

One day, a little mouse ran across a sleeping lion's paw. This woke the lion. The lion was angry at being woken up, and he grabbed the little mouse in his big paw. He was about to eat the mouse when the mouse said, "Please don't eat me. If you will let me go, I will find a way to help you someday."

The lion laughed. He thought that such a small mouse could never help a great lion like himself. But, he let the mouse go. Not long after this, the mouse was running through the forest and heard a loud roaring. He saw the lion, who was trapped in a hunter's net. The mouse remembered how the lion had let him go. He ran to the net and began chewing at the ropes. Soon, he had made a hole big enough for the lion to get free.

– adapted from the fable by Aesop

The lion thought that an animal as small as the mouse could never help one as big as himself. Then, he got trapped in a net. Though he was big, he could not get out. The mouse, though small, was able to do what the lion could not. The mouse saved the lion's life. The lesson of this fable is that little friends may be great friends.

Practice 2: Lessons in Literature

ELA4R1h Lit

Read the passages below. Then, answer the questions.

The Fox and the Crow

A fox saw a crow sitting in a tree with a piece of cheese in her beak.

"I want that cheese," thought the fox. So, he went to the foot of the tree.

"Hello, Crow," he cried. "How well you are looking today! Your feathers are so glossy! Your eyes are so bright! You must be a good singer as well. Could I hear you sing just one song?"

The crow was pleased by the nice things the fox said. She wanted to sing so the fox would praise her voice too. But, when she opened her beak, the piece of cheese fell to the ground. The fox quickly snapped it up.

"Thank you!" he cried. "In exchange for your cheese I will give you a piece of advice for the future: _____."

– adapted from the fable by Aesop

---

1. What did the fox say at the end of this story? (What is the lesson that should fill in the blank?)

   A. "Always try to be the first person to eat."

   B. "Do not share your food with anyone else."

   C. "It is not wise to sing to foxes, especially if you are a crow."

   D. "Do not trust people who give too many compliments."

2. How did the fox fool the crow?

   A. He sang to her and put her to sleep.

   B. He made her think she was a fox like him.

   C. He tricked her to get something from her.

   D. He climbed up and stole the food from her.

The Tortoise and the Hare

Once there was a hare, who was always bragging about how fast he could run. "I dare anyone to try to beat me!" he said.

The tortoise said quietly, "I will race you."

"Ha!" said the hare. "Everyone knows that you are slow. You will never beat a runner like me."

"We'll see," said the tortoise. "Let's race."

The race began. The hare was soon far ahead of the tortoise. He knew it, so he stopped and said, "I am so far ahead that I have time to take a nap. I'll have plenty of time to wake up and still win the race."

The hare went to sleep. He slept when the tortoise walked by him. He woke up just in time to see the tortoise cross the finish line to win the race!

– adapted from the fable by Aesop

---

3. Why did the tortoise win the race?

   A. He focused on the goal.   C. He scared the hare.

   B. He practiced harder.   D. He cheated.

4. What is the lesson in this story?

   A. Someone who runs fast will always win the important races.

   B. The person who boasts the most wins the race.

   C. Hard work can be more important than being the best at something.

   D. Don't take a nap when you're in a competition with someone.

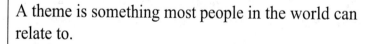

CHAPTER 10 SUMMARY

In this chapter, you read about the author's message.

A **theme** is a message about life and the way people act.

A theme is something most people in the world can relate to.

A **lesson** is a message about how we should act.

CHAPTER 10 REVIEW

ELA4R1h Lit

Read each passage. Answer the questions that follow.

> The story "The Ugly Duckling" begins with a mother duck waiting for her ducklings to hatch. When the eggs finally crack, all of the babies look as she expects, except for one. He looks different from the other ducklings. Everyone on the farm thinks he is ugly and teases him. Finally, he runs away. But, wherever he goes, he is teased because he looks different. He suffers for a long time, going from place to place as people make fun of him. He spends a cold winter alone on a frozen pond. When spring comes, he sees some beautiful birds nearby. He is so lonely that he goes to them, expecting to be teased as usual. But, the birds are friendly to him. Suddenly, he sees his reflection in the water. He realizes that he is not a duckling but a swan, just like these beautiful birds. He thinks that it was worth his suffering to be this happy.

1. What is the theme of this passage?

   A. We must find our place in the world.

   B. It is often very hard to be brave.

   C. Strangers can sometimes be unkind.

   D. True love overcomes all.

2. How does the author use the plot to show the theme?

   A. The duckling's mother had to wait for him to hatch.

   B. The ugly duckling spent the winter alone on a pond.

   C. Until he finds his true family, the duckling is teased.

   D. Swans turn out to be much friendlier than ducks are.

Little Red Riding Hood

There was once a girl named Little Red Riding Hood. She lived with her mother in the woods. One day, her mother asked her to take some cakes to her grandmother, who was sick in bed. It was a long walk through thick woods.

"Go quickly, stay on the path, and do not stop along the way," her mother said.

Little Red Riding Hood took the cakes and started through the woods. Soon, she met a wolf. The hungry wolf thought he would like to eat both the girl and her grandmother. He convinced her to stop and pick some flowers a little way off the path.

While she was busy, the wolf hurried ahead to the grandmother's house. He ate up the grandmother, and then tucked himself under the covers to wait for Little Red Riding Hood. When she came, he quickly ate her as well, and then lay down for a nap.

A passing hunter heard the snores and came to check on the grandmother. He was able to save both the girl and her grandmother. Little Red Riding Hood thought, "After this, I will always do as my mother tells me and never leave the path again."

– adapted from the folktale as told by the Brothers Grimm

3. Why does Little Red Riding Hood get into trouble?

   A. She leaves the path.

   B. She eats the cakes.

   C. She runs away.

   D. She hits the wolf.

4. What is the theme of this story?

   A. It is best to be friendly.

   B. Don't be greedy.

   C. Obey your parents.

   D. Have courage.

The Dog with His Master's Dinner

A dog had been taught to carry his master's dinner in a basket. Every day, the dog carried the dinner to the place where his master worked. He was an honest dog and never stole a bit of it. One day, a pack of dog thieves stole the basket. They began to eat up the dinner as fast as they could. The poor dog tried and tried to get his master's dinner back, but he could not. At last, he said to himself, "Well, if the dinner must be stolen, I may as well have my share too." The dog began to eat just as fast as the rest. In a minute or two, all the dinner was eaten. The dog's hungry master, who was working in the field, waited for it in vain.

– adapted from *Rock A Bye Library: A Book of Fables* (author unknown)

5. What is the lesson?

   A. Eat when you are hungry.

   B. Do what everyone else is doing.

   C. Two wrongs do not make a right.

   D. You should make the best of a bad situation.

6. What would the author want to say to the dog?

   A. "You should have bitten the dog thieves."

   B. "You did the best that you could."

   C. "You should have made your master more food."

   D. "You should have run away forever."

Honest George Washington

George Washington, our first president, was well-known to be an honest man. Legend has it that when he was a boy, George got a hatchet for a gift. After practicing on some logs, George thought it would be fun to chop down a real tree. Without thinking, he cut down one of his father's prized cherry trees. His father was angry when he saw the tree. He asked George if he had done it. Though he knew his father was angry, George told the truth.

"Yes, Father," he said. "I cannot tell a lie. I did cut down the tree."

George's father was sorry to lose the tree. He was also proud of George for telling the truth.

---

7. What is the lesson?

   A. Don't cut down trees without permission.

   B. Kids should not play with hatchets.

   C. Actions have consequences.

   D. Always tell the truth.

8. If you broke a plate, what would young George most likely tell you to do?

   A. Hide the pieces.

   B. Blame someone else.

   C. Tell your parents.

   D. Run and hide in your room.

George Washington

Chapter 11
Literature and an Author's Life

This chapter addresses the following GPS-based CRCT standard(s):

ELA4R1 The student demonstrates comprehension and shows evidence of a warranted and responsible explanation of a variety of literary and informational texts.

For literary texts, the student identifies the characteristics of various genres and produces evidence of reading that:

g. Identifies similarities and differences between the characters or events and theme in a literary work and the actual experiences in an author's life.

Do you know someone who wants to be a pro football player? That person probably loves football. Some people turn things they love as a child into things they do for work when they grow up. In the same way, authors sometimes takes things from their own lives and use them in their stories.

WHY AUTHORS WRITE

Why does a writer write? Some writers have a story to tell. Some want to share a part of themselves with the world. Some want to share the unique way they see things. Whatever the reason, most writing can be broken down into three main types. Writers write to inform, to persuade, and to entertain.

Writers of literature usually write to entertain. These writers have stories that they think we will enjoy. Maybe we will learn more about ourselves. Maybe we will see how we are like a character in the story. Maybe we will feel that there are others like us.

Author Beverly Cleary wrote because she saw a need for a certain kind of book. When she was young, she wanted to read books about children like herself. She had a hard time finding books like that. When she worked as a children's librarian, she found that children still wanted books about children like themselves. So, she wrote some. The result was books like her Henry Huggins and Ramona series. Cleary's stories have "real" elements that she herself looked for as a young reader. Her books are told from a child's point of view. Her characters talk about how grownups can be unfair. They complain about having to share and get along with others. Cleary writes stories that real kids can relate to.

EXPERIENCES IN AN AUTHOR'S LIFE

A writer's life can affect what he or she writes. Places to which a writer travels, things that happen, and people the writer meets can all become part of the stories.

SETTING

A writer often writes about places he or she knows. Beverly Cleary grew up in Oregon. Oregon is the setting for her books.

Writer Rudyard Kipling was born in India. His parents were British. Many of the stories Kipling wrote are set in India. Having lived there, Kipling knew what India was like.

Kipling knows India, so he writes about India. In the passage below, Kipling describes some of the creatures he came to know while living in India.

Rudyard Kipling

> So, Baloo taught him the wood and water laws. He learned how to tell a rotten branch from a sound one. He learned how to speak politely to the wild bees when he came upon a hive of them fifty feet above ground. He learned what to say to Mang the Bat when he disturbed him in the branches at midday. He learned how to warn the water snakes in the pools before he splashed down among them.
>
> – adapted from "Kaa's Hunting" in *The Jungle Book* by Rudyard Kipling

Practice 1: Setting

ELA4R1g Lit

> Mark Twain was born in Missouri and moved as a child to Mississippi. Looking for work, he moved around. He lived in New York, Ohio, and even Nevada. Later, he traveled the world and wrote about many places and things. His most famous stories are about Tom Sawyer and Huck Finn, two boys growing up in the South.

1. Why do you think that people might like Twain's stories about the South best?

   A. Stories about the South are always more fun.

   B. Twain knew the South best because he grew up there.

   C. They are funnier than Twain's other stories.

   D. Twain's life was too busy after he moved from the South.

2. Authors write some of what happens to them into their stories. What is the most likely way that Mark Twain is like one of his characters?

   A. Like Tom Sawyer, Twain grew up in Missouri.

   B. Like Aunt Polly, Twain became a loving parent.

   C. Like Huckleberry Finn, he was always in trouble.

   D. Like Huck's friend Jim, he ran away from slavery.

PLOT

Things that happen to a writer often make their way into a story. If an author moved often or lost a parent at a young age, these things might show up in a book.

When writer Roald Dahl was in school, he got to test chocolates. A chocolate company sent boxes of new kinds of chocolates to his school. The kids would taste test the chocolates. Dahl wanted to invent a new chocolate bar. He wanted to impress the owner of Cadbury's chocolate company. He used this idea later in his book *Charlie and the Chocolate Factory*.

Dahl turned this event into a story. Sometimes, a writer turns her life into a story. Author Louisa May Alcott grew up in a poor family. She was one of four sisters. The family was smart, but they never had much money. Alcott's book *Little Women* is based on her experiences as a child.

Do you see some of Alcott's own life in this passage from *Little Women*?

> "Christmas won't be Christmas without any presents," grumbled Jo, lying on the rug.
>
> "It's so dreadful to be poor!" sighed Meg, looking down at her old dress.
>
> "I don't think it's fair for some girls to have plenty of pretty things, and other girls nothing at all," added little Amy, with an injured sniff.
>
> "We've got Father and Mother, and each other," said Beth contentedly from her corner.
>
> – from *Little Women* by Louisa May Alcott

Practice 2: Plot

ELA4R1g Lit

1. In the passage from *Little Women*, does the author show how she felt about being poor?

   A. She tells how everything is all right as long as the family is together.

   B. She shows that it's horrible because Christmas is ruined.

   C. She has each sister tell a little about what it's like.

   D. She depicts the pain the faces of the girls.

2. Louisa May Alcott is said to be most like the character Jo in this book. Jo is an active girl, is very outspoken, and loves to write. From the passage, what else can be said about Jo?

   A. She is very friendly little girl.

   B. She likes exchanging gifts.

   C. She wants a new dress.

   D. She loves her sisters dearly.

CHARACTERS

A writer may also include characters based on friends or family. Author Beatrix Potter had few friends as a child, but many pets. Two of her favorites were her rabbits, Benjamin and Peter. She watched them carefully and took them on walks. She played with them, drew pictures of them, and knew them well. She used both of these pets as characters in her stories, *The Tale of Benjamin Bunny* and *The Tale of Peter Rabbit*.

Here is a part of her story, *The Tale of Peter Rabbit*.

> Flopsy, Mopsy and Cotton-tail, who were good little bunnies, went down the lane together to gather blackberries.
>
> But Peter, who was very naughty, ran straight away to Mr. McGregor's garden and squeezed under the gate!

What can you guess about her pet rabbit, Peter?

If you guessed he was mischievous, then you're right!

Practice 3: Characters

ELA4R1g Lit

> The famous storyteller Aesop wrote many fables. Fables, as you know, teach us lessons about how to act. They often have animals as the main characters, but they talk about how people should behave. Not very much is known about Aesop, but many say he was born a slave and that he was ugly and deformed.

1. If this is true about Aesop, what is a likely reason that he wrote many of his fables?

   A. He was treated badly and wanted to get back at people.

   B. He wanted to stand up for others like himself.

   C. He tried to show people that animals have feelings too.

   D. He met many people who looked like animals.

2. What is MOST likely a reason Aesop used animals as his characters?

   A. Animals have more adventures than humans do.

   B. Humans can learn from the animals in the stories.

   C. Humans don't need to learn lessons, but animals do.

   D. Animals provide hours of entertainment for humans.

THEME

Sometimes a writer uses ideas about life in his writing. You read earlier about Rudyard Kipling. Kipling was an English boy who was born in India. His parents were British citizens who lived in India. Kipling lived in India until he was six, when he returned to England. While in India, Kipling mostly spoke the native language. He had to remember to speak English. But, he was an English boy and looked like an English boy. This must have made him wonder who he really was. Was he English, like his parents? Or was he Indian, like everyone else in the country that he knew?

Kipling wrote a book called *Kim,* which is about a white boy living in India. The theme in *Kim* of "Who am I?" comes from Kipling's own life. Read the passage from Kim below.

> Kim was black as any native. He chose to speak the Indian language. His English was clipped and uncertain. Though he was friendly and equal with the Indian boys at the bazaar, Kim was white—a poor white of the very poorest.
>
> – adapted from *Kim*, by Rudyard Kipling

What is the same in it as in Kipling's life? Part of Kim comes from his family and part of him comes from where he lives. Is he really Indian or English? He is a mix of the two, just as Kipling himself was.

Practice 4: Theme

ELA4R1g Lit

1. The Brothers Grimm are famous for writing down many folktales. They were scholars who loved old stories and wanted to record them for future generations. When they were kids, they lived a life of luxury. Then, their father died. This left their mother struggling to raise them. She had to be strict. Times became harder for the brothers. Life with their father was much more fun than it was after their father was gone. Which theme in some fairytales reflects their experience?

   A. Stepmothers can be wicked.

   B. We all have fairy godmothers.

   C. Forest animals may be evil creatures.

   D. Magical beings grant wishes to the poor.

2. From what you have read about the Brothers Grimm, which of the following would MOST likely be a theme in many of their stories?

   A. the importance of wealth

   B. the importance of family

   C. the importance of eating well

   D. the importance of education

As you can see, all of the experiences in authors' lives can influence their stories. What authors do and see and who they meet can show up in their characters, plots, and settings. The theme, or underlying meaning, of any story is also affected by on how its author sees the world. Now, here is some more practice with picking out how an author's life shows up in the stories you read.

Practice 5: Influences of a Writer's Life

ELA4R1g Lit

Read the passages below. Then, answer the questions that follow.

> You read earlier about Rudyard Kipling. Here is a passage from his story about *Rikki-Tikki-Tavi*, a mongoose. The story is set in India.
>
> Then Rikki-tikki went out into the garden to see what was to be seen. It was a large garden, only half cultivated, with bushes, as big as summer-houses, of Marshal Niel roses, lime and orange trees, clumps of bamboos, and thickets of high grass.
>
> – from *Rikki-Tikki-Tavi* by Rudyard Kipling

1. How did Kipling know what an Indian garden would look like?

   A. He made it all up.

   B. He read about it in a book.

   C. He asked his sister about it.

   D. He lived in India as a child.

Mongoose

2. If Kipling had been born in England, how might the setting have been different?

   A. He could have made the flowers different colors.

   B. He could have used different plants and animals.

   C. The story would have been the same either way.

   D. The story would have been happier if it were set in England.

Writer Anna Sewell had an accident when she was young. It left her unable to walk or stand. She used a horse and cart to get around. She was with horses all the time and depended on them to move. This made her love horses. Anna Sewell is the author of *Black Beauty*, a famous horse story. Now, read the passage from *Black Beauty*.

You have been well-bred and well-born; your father has a great name in these parts, and your grandfather won the cup at the races; your grandmother had the sweetest temper of any horse I ever knew, and I think you have never seen me kick or bite. I hope you will grow up gentle and good, and never learn bad ways; do your work with a good will, lift your feet up well when you trot, and never bite or kick even in play.

– from *Black Beauty Young Folks' Edition* by Anna Sewell

3. Why did Sewell write about horses?
   A. She knew them well.
   B. She wished she had one.
   C. She liked to draw them.
   D. She was scared of them.

4. What does Sewell seem to think about horses?
   A. They are useful animals.
   B. They bite and kick.
   C. They are like people.
   D. They are lazy.

CHAPTER 11 SUMMARY

Authors write for many reasons.

Writers' experiences can affect what they write. Things that happen to writers, the people they meet, and the places they go can all show up in their stories.

CHAPTER 11 REVIEW

ELA4R1g Lit

Read the passages that follow. Then, answer the questions.

> Hans Christian Andersen was not like other kids. He had a learning disability, which made school difficult for him. He was older than his classmates were. They teased him and did not accept him.
>
> Hans Christian Andersen wrote "Thumbelina." It is the story of a tiny girl. She lives in a world where everyone else is normal-sized. Her bed, her toys, and everything else she needs all must be adapted from a big person's world. There is no one her size. She has a series of adventures, all challenging because of her size. At the end, she finds and marries someone who is the same size as she.

1. What makes Thumbelina different?

   A. She cannot read or write.

   B. She is smaller than everyone else.

   C. She has a very large head.

   D. She speaks a different language.

2. What is the theme of the story?

   A. being an outsider

   B. being the best

   C. losing a parent

   D. being courageous

3. What do Thumbelina and Andersen have in common?

   A. Neither could read nor write.

   B. Neither fit into their world.

   C. Both liked baseball.

   D. Both were fast runners.

Hans Christian Andersen also wrote "The Ugly Duckling." "The Ugly Duckling" tells the story of a young bird who is teased all the time. He is teased because he looks different from everyone else. In the end, he finds that he is not a duckling but a swan. He finds love and acceptance once he finds others like himself.

4. Based on the description you read of Andersen's life, who is the ugly duckling in his story?

   A. his mother

   B. his brother

   C. his pet duck

   D. himself

Joel Chandler Harris was born in Georgia before the Civil War. He gathered stories he heard from slaves. He called the collections his Uncle Remus stories. Uncle Remus is a character who tells these stories. Now, read the passage from *Nights with Uncle Remus* below.

It had been raining all day so that Uncle Remus found it impossible to go out. The storm had begun, the old man declared, just as the chickens were crowing for day, and it had continued almost without intermission. The dark gray clouds had blotted out the sun, and the leafless limbs of the tall oaks surrendered themselves drearily to the fantastic gusts that drove the drizzle fitfully before them. The lady to whom Uncle Remus belonged had been thoughtful of the old man, and 'Tildy, the house-girl, had been commissioned to carry him his meals. This arrangement came to the knowledge of the little boy at supper time, and he lost no time in obtaining permission to accompany 'Tildy.

– adapted from "Mr. Fox and Miss Goose" in *Nights with Uncle Remus*
by Joel Chandler Harris

5. What can you tell about Uncle Remus?

   A. He is a slave.

   B. He owns slaves.

   C. He is the President.

   D. He is a fisherman.

6. What is the setting?

    A. an apartment in New York

    B. a wagon in the West

    C. a farm in the South

    D. a car on the highway

7. Why did Harris likely collect these stories?

    A. He couldn't think of his own.

    B. He heard and enjoyed them growing up.

    C. He wanted to hide them from other people.

    D. He thought they were frightening.

Joel Chandler Harris

Chapter 12
Media in Our Lives

This chapter addresses the following GPS-based CRCT standard(s):

ELA4LSV2 The student listens to and views various forms of text and media in order to gather and share information, persuade others, and express and understand ideas.

When responding to visual and oral texts and media (e.g., television, radio, film productions, and electronic media), the student:

a. Demonstrates an awareness of the presence of the media in the daily lives of most people.

b. Evaluates the role of the media in focusing attention and in forming an opinion.

c. Judges the extent to which the media provides a source of entertainment was well as a source of information.

Did you watch TV last night? Did you read a sign on a bus? Did you listen to the radio? TV, signs, and radio are all examples of **media**. Media is any written, spoken, or printed way to present a message to many people. Media is everywhere.

KINDS OF MEDIA

We see all kinds of media each day. Media can be something you read. Magazines and newspapers are media. You also can watch or listen to media. Radio and TV are media. Any way to reach many people at one time can be media.

On the next page are some common types of media. Did you read, see, or hear any of these today?

Kinds of Media	
Kind	**Examples**
television	a news report about a fire an ad for a new video game
Internet	an e-mail from a store about a sale an online banner ad for MP3 players
radio	a sports talk program an ad for a car wash
magazine	a story about solar power an ad for an American Girl doll
newspaper	an article about the city's budget an ad for a local store opening
billboards, posters	a billboard for a new cell phone posters for movies playing in theaters

Practice 1: Kinds of Media
ELA4LSV2a

1. Which of the following is NOT an example of media?

    A. a weather report on TV

    B. a music video

    C. your school newspaper

    D. a call from a friend

2. Where would you MOST likely see an ad telling you to buy candy, soda, and popcorn?

    A. at a movie theatre

    B. on a bus

    C. on the Internet

    D. on the radio

3. Which of these types of media could an adult use while driving a car?

    A. magazine   B. movie   C. radio   D. Internet

4. Which type of media might you see while riding on a bus?

    A. a poster

    B. a newspaper

    C. a magazine

    D. any of the above

WHAT MEDIA DOES

Media is used for different reasons.

- Media can be used to **inform**.

  A newspaper prints facts to inform the reader.

- Media can be used to **persuade**.

  A toy company uses ads to persuade kids to buy toys.

- Media can be used to **entertain**.

  A sitcom on TV entertains an audience.

You should be aware of what media is trying to do. You also need to know what it is trying to get you to do. When you know the purpose, you can learn things about the message. Read on to find out how media informs, persuades, and entertains.

TO INFORM

Media that **informs** gives facts about a topic. Experts might tell you facts. Doctors and scientists are experts who most people trust. A cooking show can also inform. A video that shows you how to build a birdhouse informs too.

Graphics can make the facts easier to understand. Pictures make stories more fun to read. Diagrams show you how to put together an item. Photographs can show you how a finished project looks.

Read the following passage. The author's purpose is to inform.

> Claude Monet was a famous painter. He painted many landscapes. His water lily paintings are very bright. He painted them in his garden in France.

Media that informs can also **focus attention** on issues. For an issue to be fixed, people need to know about it. For example, Georgia sometimes suffers from drought. Georgians can learn about droughts from the media. A TV news report might tell how to make a rain barrel. A Web site might show pictures of a dry lake. Media brings attention to the problem. This helps people understand. It shows people what they can do about a problem.

TO PERSUADE

Media that **persuades** wants you to change your mind or what you are doing. Ads are a good example of media that persuades. Advertisers try to make you want an item. They might do this by telling you how their product is better than others.

Media that persuades uses different ways to do so. Here are some of the ways media persuades.

How Media Persuades		
Type	**Definition**	**Example**
experts	getting an expert to tell us to buy something can persuade us	A doctor on TV tells you to take the vitamin he is selling.
repetition	saying or singing something over and over so we will remember it	A car dealer repeats a price many times.
bandwagon	saying that you will be left out if you don't act	A toy company says that everyone will have this toy, so you should too.
vagueness	making claims that are hard to prove	A dish liquid is claimed to be "the best."

Media that persuades can also help us to **form an opinion**. We can listen to different people's ideas. Then, we can decide what we think about an issue. For instance, a person running for a political office gives a speech. He tells us why his ideas are best. A campaign ad tells us why we should not trust the other candidate. We listen to what these people have to say, and we decide whom to believe.

TO ENTERTAIN

Media that **entertains** is for fun. Books entertain. Movies, cartoons, and music entertain.

The author's purpose in the passage below is to entertain.

Jen snuck around the corner of the house. She was holding a water balloon. She heard the door open. She knew it was her brother, so she threw the balloon. Oh no! It was her father! He was soaked and very surprised, but luckily, he was not mad.

Now you know the three purposes of media. When you see media, you can ask, "What is the purpose?"

- If the purpose is to inform, you know you are about to hear some facts.
- If the purpose is to persuade, you know that someone is trying to get you to do something.
- If the purpose is to entertain, you can enjoy the show.

Some messages are believable. Some are not. Knowing a writer's purpose can help you understand how media relates to you. You can figure out what to do with the messages you see each day.

Practice 2: What Media Does

ELA4LSV2b, c

Read the passages that follow. Then, answer the questions.

> *AllSports II* is a new video game for kids just like you. If you like sports, and if you like video games, *AllSports II* is for you. It is just $29.99. Find it at any store.

1. What is the purpose of the passage above?

   A. to inform

   B. to entertain

   C. to persuade

   D. to focus attention

Bees are important. They make honey, which we use to sweeten many foods and drinks. They have another big job too. Bees spread pollen as they visit flowers. This helps more flowers grow.

2. What is the purpose of the passage above?
   A. to inform
   B. to entertain

   C. to persuade
   D. to focus attention

My family likes to tell a story about when we got our dog, Mutt. We all went to the rescue center together. We walked from cage to cage, looking at the dogs. One stood out from all the rest. Every time one of us got near him, he rolled over on his back, wagged his tail, and howled the saddest howl you've ever heard. We knew he needed us, so we brought him home. Now, any time he does something wrong, he does the same thing. He knows we can't stay mad at him when he does that!

3. What is the purpose of the passage above?
   A. to inform
   B. to entertain
   C. to persuade
   D. to focus attention

> I'm a doctor. Smoking cigarettes is bad for your lungs.

4. What is the purpose of the passage above?

   A. to persuade

   B. to entertain

   C. to focus attention

   D. to inform

> I'm a doctor. Try these new vitamin supplements I have invented! They are the best.

5. What is the purpose of the passage above?

   A. to inform

   B. to persuade

   C. to entertain

   D. to focus attention

> This model car is only $9.99. It looks just like a real car. And, it can be yours for just $9.99. Its doors and trunk open. Call now to get your car for just $9.99. Remember, that's just $9.99!

6. Which technique did the ad use to persuade?

   A. experts

   B. repetition

   C. bandwagon

   D. vagueness

When gas prices rise, news reports show price increases. Web sites tell us how to conserve gas. Car dealerships advertise free gas for buying a new car.

7. What do these different media reports do?

A. form an opinion

B. persuade

C. entertain

D. focus attention

Two people want to be president. One tells us that the best way to take care of the elderly is to cut taxes. The other tells us that the best way to take care of the elderly is to raise taxes.

8. By listening to these two people, what can you do?

A. form an opinion

B. persuade someone else

C. entertain the elderly

D. focus attention on yourself

CHAPTER 12 SUMMARY

In this chapter, you learned about the media. Media is part of our daily lives. Some kinds of media we often see are the Internet, television, and magazines.

Media has different purposes.

- Media can be used to **inform**—to give facts about a topic. Media that informs can also **focus attention** on an issue.

- Media can be used to **persuade**—to get you to change your mind or your actions. Media can persuade by using experts, repetition, bandwagon, and vagueness. Media that persuades can also help us **form an opinion**.

- Media can be used to **entertain**—for fun.

It is important to find out what the purpose is. Then, you can decide how to use media.

CHAPTER 12 REVIEW

ELA4LSV2a, b, c

Read the passages that follow. Then, answer the questions.

> George Washington was our first president. He is remembered as "the father of our country."

1. What is the purpose of the passage above?

    A. to inform

    B. to entertain

    C. to persuade

    D. to get attention

If you elect me to be class president, I will make changes to this school. I will work to get us better lunches. I will get us longer recess. If you elect me, I will get these jobs done.

2. What is the purpose of the passage above?

A. to inform

B. to entertain

C. to persuade

D. to get attention

 If you don't buy these sneakers, everyone will make laugh at you. They will say that you don't know fashion. Get your mom to buy these so you will look like everyone else.

3. Which technique did the ad above use?

A. experts

B. repetition

C. bandwagon

D. vagueness

It is important to brush your teeth after eating candy. The best toothpaste to use is Smile-o-dent. As a dentist, I highly recommend this brand. I tell all of my patients to use it.

4. Which technique did the ad above use?

A. experts

B. repetition

C. bandwagon

D. vagueness

5. Which type of media might you find in a recycling bin?

   A. a newspaper

   B. the Internet

   C. a radio show

   D. a TV program

6. Which type of media does not broadcast sound?

   A. radio

   B. television

   C. a movie

   D. a newspaper

After a storm destroys a city, photos on a Web site show wrecked homes. News reports show businesses donating food to help.

---

7. What do these different media reports do?

   A. inform

   B. persuade

   C. entertain

   D. focus attention

"Please come to the movie with me, Janie!" Marcella begged. "It's going to be so cute! It's got Zac Efron in it! There's supposed to be a lot of great scenery from Hawaii! Did I mention Zac Efron is in it? I heard that he sings, like, ten songs! It's going to be so good! Come on! It's got Zac Efron as the star, so why wouldn't it be good?"

---

8. What method did Marcella use to try to persuade Janie?

   A. experts

   B. repetition

   C. bandwagon

   D. vagueness

Mastering the Georgia 4th Grade CRCT in Reading

Practice Test 1

The purpose of this practice test is to measure your knowledge in reading comprehension. This practice test is based on the Georgia Performance Standards for reading and adheres to the sample question format provided by the Georgia Department of Education.

General Directions:

1. Read all directions carefully.

2. Read each question or sample. Then choose the best answer.

3. Choose only one answer for each question. If you change an answer, be sure to erase your original answer completely.

Section 1

A Puzzling Problem

How do you send a gift that stands 151 feet tall and weighs 225 tons? This was a problem the French people faced. They wanted to give the United States the tallest gift it had ever received.

A man named Edouard de Laboulaye had an idea. He wanted a statue made. It would show two things that were important to both France and the United States—their friendship and freedom. Many people agreed with him. They wanted to help with the project. They began raising money to pay for this special gift. Then, they hired a sculptor. Frederic Auguste Bartholdi drew a sketch of the statue. Then, he made a small model of his design. He named it *Liberty Enlightening the World*. Today, most people call it the *Statue of Liberty* or *Lady Liberty*.

It took many years to raise the money for the statue. After that, it was time to build. Many people worked to construct the iron frame and copper skin of the statue. Their hard work was rewarded. In July of 1884, the statue was complete.

The United States had agreed to build the pedestal for the statue. They would build it on Bedloe's Island, now called Liberty Island. The island is in the New York harbor. The statue was in Paris. There were more than 3600 miles and an ocean between the statue and its base!

Bartholdi had a plan. Back in France, men began taking the statue apart. They carefully marked each piece. That way the statue could be put back together correctly in New York. Next, they had to pack the 350 pieces for the trip. Bartholdi had 214 special cases made to carry the parts. Some of the filled cases only weighed a few hundred pounds. Other cases weighed thousands of pounds. Once the cases were filled, the people moved them onto a ship called the *Isere*. The *Isere* carried its precious cargo across the rough seas. The trip took twenty-seven days.

The ship was greeted with disappointing news. When it arrived on June 17, 1885, the pedestal was not built. The statue had to remain in pieces until April of the next year. Once the Americans finished building the base, the Frenchmen went to work. They started putting the statue back together like pieces of a giant puzzle. It took four months to finish the task.

1. How tall is the statue? 4R1a Inf

   A. 151 feet

   B. 214 feet

   C. 225 feet

   D. 350 feet

2. Why did the French 4R1e Inf people wait so long to start building the statue?

   A. There was not enough money.

   B. There were not enough workers.

   C. There was no design for the statue.

   D. They had to wait for the copper to arrive.

3. Which is the BEST 4R1f Inf summary of the last paragraph?

   A. Building the statue was like putting together a puzzle.

   B. The French were disappointed when they arrived in New York.

   C. The Statue of Liberty stayed in hundreds of pieces for more than a year after it arrived in the United States.

   D. French workers had to wait for Americans to make the pedestal, before starting the four-month job of putting the statue back together.

4. What pair of words in the 4R3i passage MOST closely mean the same thing?

   A. sketch, model

   B. statue, puzzle

   C. construct, build

   D. friendship, freedom

5. Why did they ship the 4R1g Inf statue in many pieces?

   A. It was too tall for the ship.

   B. It was too heavy for the ship.

   C. They knew the base would not be ready on time.

   D. They knew the cases would protect it from the salt water.

The Shoes

Click

Clack

Click

Clack

The students all strain to hear.

Click

Clack

Click

Clack

That familiar sound is very clear.

Click

Clack

Click

Clack

The principal's feet are what we fear.

Tap

Tap

Tap

Tap

Do we dare to take a look?

Ahem

Ahem

Ahem

Ahem

The news is good; she brought a book!

6. Which pair of words from the poem rhyme? 4R1i Lit

A. click, clack

B. hear, clear

C. fear, look

D. tap, ahem

7. The author uses the words *click clack* so the reader will 4R1i Lit

A. hear the footsteps.

B. guess who is coming.

C. see the worried students.

D. understand the problem.

8. The poem is told from the point of view of 4R1c Lit

A. the shoes.

B. the narrator.

C. the principal.

D. the students.

9. As it is used in the poem, the word *strain* means 4R3h

A. to pull or hurt a muscle.

B. to sort or remove parts.

C. to make strong efforts.

D. to make more difficult.

10. The poem takes place in a 4R1b Lit

A. house.

B. school.

C. shoe store.

D. playground.

Three Sisters

Long ago and far away lived three sisters: Hannah, Anna, and Diana. One day, Hannah saw her neighbor had accidently spilled his wheat seeds. Hannah stopped to help gather the neighbor's seeds; in appreciation, the farmer removed a handful of seeds from his sack. "Plant these," he said, "and you'll enjoy the finest bread you've ever tasted."

When Hannah arrived home, she showed her sisters the seeds. "Who will help plant the seeds?" she asked.

"Not us," her sisters said.

"Then I will do it myself," Hannah said. She carried the seeds into the field, turned the earth over repeatedly, and planted the seeds. Months passed as the seeds drank up the sunshine and the rain and turned from seeds to green plants to tall wheat stalks. When the wheat was as golden as the hair on Hannah's head, Hannah called her sisters to the field. "Who will help gather the wheat?" she asked.

"Not us," her sisters said.

"Then I will do it myself," Hannah said. So, Hannah cut the wheat stalks and removed the kernels of golden wheat. She placed the wheat kernels in a basket and carried the basket into the house. She showed her sisters the golden treasure and asked, "Who will help carry this wheat to the miller?"

"Not us," her sisters said.

"Then I will do it myself," Hannah said. The next morning, Hannah lifted the heavy basket onto her hip and traveled by foot to the grain mill. When she returned, she showed her sisters the sack of freshly ground flour. "Now, who will help bake this flour into bread?"

"Not us," her sisters said.

"Then I will do it myself," Hannah said. Hannah measured and mixed and kneaded and shaped until she had a perfectly shaped loaf of bread in the oven. Soon, the tiny cottage filled with the smell of baking bread. When Hannah was ready to take the bread from the oven, her sisters appeared in the kitchen. As Hannah pulled out the golden brown loaves, she asked, "Now, who will help eat the bread?" Before her sisters could answer, Hannah said, "I planted the seeds and cut the wheat by myself. I carried the wheat to the miller by myself, and I baked the bread by myself. Now, I shall eat the bread by myself." She found it to be very tasty too!

11. Who is telling the story?   4R1c Lit

A. Hannah

B. the narrator

C. the neighbor

D. Hannah's sisters

12. What word BEST describes Hannah's sisters?   4R1b Lit

A. lazy

B. young

C. helpful

D. curious

13. Which phrase from the story is a metaphor?   4R1d Lit

A. spilled his wheat seeds

B. seeds drank up the sunshine

C. as golden as the hair on Hannah's head

D. showed her sisters the golden treasure

14. Readers could predict who would bake the bread because   4R1e Lit

A. Hannah did not like to work with others.

B. the sisters had not helped with any of the work.

C. bread is the only thing you can make with wheat.

D. the farmer told Hannah the bread would taste good.

15. What lesson is found in the story?   4R1h Lit

A. Hard work is justly rewarded.

B. Good things come from sharing.

C. Everyone is happy when everyone helps.

D. It is best for each of us to speak for ourselves.

Boomerangs

Throwing a boomerang and having it return to you is a skill which requires much practice. You will use both your mind and your body when you learn this sport.

Where?

The first question to ask yourself when choosing a practice spot is, "Is it safe?" A boomerang is a hard wooden object that moves through the air quickly. You cannot always predict where it will go. You need to protect yourself and others from injuries. Find an open area without trees, streetlights, or houses. You need at least 180 feet of open space all around you. Parks are often good choices.

When?

The key to being safe is to always keep your eye on the boomerang. That means no night flying. Snow is also a problem for boomerangs. If your boomerang comes in low, it can cut into the snow and travel for many feet under the surface. Instead of spending your time throwing and catching, you will spend your time digging and searching. A sunny day with a light breeze is the perfect weather for the sport.

How?

Always throw a boomerang overhand like a baseball. There are two basic grips. The first grip is called the pinch. Pinch one end of the boomerang between your thumb and forefinger. Snap your wrist at the end of the throw, releasing the boomerang and creating some spin on it. The second grip is called the cradle. Start with the pinch grip and slide your forefinger around to the front of the boomerang. When you snap your wrist, pull back on your "trigger finger" to create spin. Try each grip to see which one helps you create more spin.

The most exciting part of the toss is the catch. If the boomerang is below your shoulder level, use a two-handed catch. Reach out and clap, catching the boomerang between your hands. If the boomerang is coming in higher, raise one arm, and reach into the hole formed by the spinning boomerang. Think of it as the eye of a tornado. When your hand is in place, grab the boomerang. Be careful! The boomerang might bounce off of your hand and quickly change directions.

Why?

Throwing a boomerang can be great fun. In the beginning stages, it also provides plenty of exercise. You will find yourself running all over the open field to recover the boomerang when it doesn't return to you!

16. What is the concluding sentence in "Where?"   4R1b Inf

   A. You cannot always predict where it will go.

   B. You need to protect yourself and others from injuries.

   C. You need at least 180 feet of open space all around you.

   D. Parks are often good choices.

17. Why do you snap your wrist at the end of a throw?   4R1e Inf

   A. It causes the boomerang to spin.

   B. It causes people to look for the boomerang.

   C. It causes the boomerang to bounce off your hand.

   D. It causes the thrower to lose sight of the boomerang.

18. Which sentence is an opinion?   4R1h Inf

   A. You need to protect yourself and others from injuries.

   B. Snow is also a problem for boomerangs.

   C. There are two basic grips.

   D. The most exciting part of the toss is the catch.

19. The word *skill* means   4R3b

   A. a fun sport.

   B. a wooden object.

   C. a learned ability to do something well.

   D. a safe way of playing or exercising alone.

20. The passage is organized in   4R1d Inf

   A. chronological order.

   B. cause and effect order.

   C. question and answer order.

   D. compare and contrast order.

Saturday Afternoon

The room was like a cave. Maya wondered what kinds of creatures she might see scooting across the floor. The thought sent a shiver up her spine. She took a deep breath and stepped further into the room. The creaking floorboards loudly announced her arrival. A woman sitting at a desk looked up over her glasses. She frowned as Maya rushed by the oversized desk. Maya kept moving until she was in a narrow aisle formed by rows of towering bookcases. The room went from dim to dark. Maya squinted to read the words on the dusty spines of the books. Her head twisted from right to left and left to right as if she was watching a tennis match. Her body jerked to attention when she heard footsteps. She spotted the woman staring down the aisle at her. Unable to calm herself, Maya grabbed two books and hurried to the desk. Without saying a word, she handed the books and her worn blue card to the woman. When the woman returned the items, Maya whispered, "Thank you." Then, she spun around on her heels and hurried to the door.

About the Author

The author recalls going to the library as a child. She loved the books and the librarian. She loved being able to walk there on her own. However, she also pictures the cold stone building and the creaky floor boards. Mostly, she remembers how much she looked forward to going there every Saturday.

21. Which is an example of personification? 4R1d Lit

   A. The room was like a cave.

   B. The creaking floorboards loudly announced her arrival.

   C. The room went from dim to dark.

   D. Maya squinted to read the words on the dusty spines of the books.

22. The setting of the story is 4R1b Lit

   A. a cave.

   B. a library.

   C. a bookstore.

   D. the woman's home.

23. How are the author and Maya alike? 4R1g Lit

   A. They both went to the library often.

   B. They both loved seeing the librarian.

   C. They both were afraid of seeing a mouse.

   D. They both had blue colored library cards.

24. Why was Maya MOST likely in a hurry to leave? 4R1f Lit

   A. She loved to spend her afternoons walking.

   B. She felt the room was too cold for her to stay.

   C. She thought the woman and the setting were scary.

   D. She was in a hurry to go home and read her books.

25. The word *unable* means 4R3e

   A. "not able."

   B. "more able."

   C. "later able."

   D. "soon able."

Section 2

Meet the New myPod: 20GB of Musical Power!

The new myPod is exactly what the world has been waiting for! Its 20 gigabytes of memory means more music at your fingertips. It's shock-proof! It's waterproof! Its extra-strong shell makes the myPod perfect for people on the go. Plus, myPod owners can enjoy the convenience of the myPod Club.* Members have unlimited use of the club site, day and night. No waiting for a store to open! At the site, members can download their favorite music. Plus, members only pay half the regular download price. There are more than 50,000 songs to choose from. New songs are added every day. Club members will never be at a loss for great music. As an added bonus, the first 100 people who bring this notice to a myPod dealer will receive a 10% discount. Plus save 10% on carrying cases and earphones! So, don't delay—check out the new myPod today!

* Membership in the myPod Club requires a one year commit-ment. A small monthly fee will be charged.

myPod

Available in six earth-friendly colors:

 sky

 soil

 grass

 sunset

 rain cloud

 blizzard

Fits in the palm of your hand!

Our competition is scared!

26. The passage is an example of   4LSV2a

    A. a how-to article.

    B. a magazine ad.

    C. a textbook page.

    D. an encyclopedia entry.

27. The purpose of the passage is to   4LSV2b

    A. sell a myPod.

    B. describe a myPod.

    C. explain how to use a myPod.

    D. show how myPod helps in sports.

28. The passage would be most helpful to someone who   4LSV2c

    A. wants to listen to music.

    B. is writing a report about music.

    C. is thinking about buying a new music player.

    D. wants to learn more about the music business.

29. If something is *convenient*, it is   4R3a

    A. easy to use.

    B. free from costs.

    C. not found nearby.

    D. needed to play music.

30. Use the dictionary entry to answer the following question.   4R3d

> **Shell** (n.) – (1) a sleeveless blouse or sweater; (2) the outside of an egg; (3) a light racing boat; (4) a thin outer covering of an object.

"Its extra strong shell makes the myPod perfect for people on the go."

The meaning of *shell* as it is used in the sentence can be found in

    A. entry 1.

    B. entry 2.

    C. entry 3.

    D. entry 4.

A Not-So-Sweet Smell

Laura inhaled. The heavy scent of chocolate filled her senses and caused her stomach to tighten. Laura knew the smell of brownies baking meant trouble. It always did. Years ago, she had learned to connect the two things. Over time, she had learned to really dislike brownies. Her mother, however, seemed to not know this.

If there had to be brownies, Laura always hoped they would be plain. Plain brownies meant small troubles. When Laura fell off her bike, a plate of brownies appeared. Then, there was her science report. Her little brother had shredded it the night before it was due. Her mother whipped up a batch of brownies and sat with her while Laura rewrote the report. Of course, Laura could not forget the glass ballerina. In her heart, she could not call that a *small* trouble, but she knew her mother did. Her mother encouraged her to eat a warm brownie *before* dinner that day. There was a hard and fast "no snack" rule before dinner in their house. Yet, less than an hour before dinnertime, Laura's mom stood before her with a plate of warm brownies and told her to enjoy one before her meal. Seconds later, her mother pulled out Laura's glass ballerina. The ballerina did not look like it was dancing any more. It was in tiny glass pieces. When Laura looked at the sparkling mountain, she knew she would never enjoy a brownie again.

Plain brownies were bad. Brownies with something extra in them were worse. They meant big trouble. In third grade, Laura's best friend moved away. Her mother told her about the upcoming move over brownies with mini-marshmallows baked into them. Then, there were the plans for a vacation in Florida. Her mother had baked a batch of brownies with raspberry jam in them. As Laura took her first cautious bite, her mother told her she had canceled their vacation.

There was no denying it. If her mother was baking brownies, trouble was on its way again. Laura tiptoed across the kitchen floor and peeked inside the small glass window on the oven door. There was the familiar baking pan. Little colored candies dotted the shiny brown top of the brownies like jewels in a crown. Laura sighed. Now what, she thought.

31. Laura does not like   4R1b Lit
    brownies because

    A. she connects them with
       trouble.

    B. she wants to be able to bake
       her own.

    C. she does not like the taste of
       chocolate.

    D. she does not like to snack
       between meals.

32. Which is a simile?   4R1d Lit

    A. batch of brownies

    B. a hard and fast rule

    C. the sparkling mountain

    D. like jewels in a crown

33. What most likely will   4R1f Lit
    happen next in the story?

    A. Laura will refuse to eat a
       brownie.

    B. Laura will finish making the
       brownies.

    C. Laura's mother will tell her
       some bad news.

    D. Laura's brother will share a
       brownie with her.

34. When Laura saw candies   4R1f Lit
    in the brownies, she felt

    A. happy.

    B. angry.

    C. worried.

    D. excited.

35. The story says Laura   4R1b Lit
    knew her mother
    thought the broken ballerina was
    a small trouble. How does she
    know this?

    A. Laura never liked the
       ballerina.

    B. Her mother baked plain
       brownies.

    C. Her mother told her it wasn't
       important.

    D. Laura knew her mother didn't
       like the ballerina.

Sea Dragons

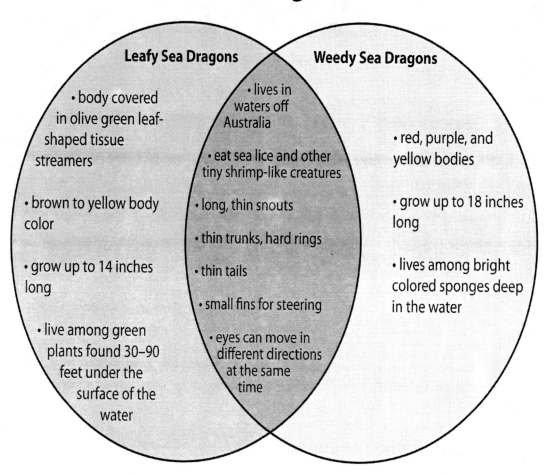

Leafy Sea Dragons

- body covered in olive green leaf-shaped tissue streamers
- brown to yellow body color
- grow up to 14 inches long
- live among green plants found 30–90 feet under the surface of the water

(shared)
- lives in waters off Australia
- eat sea lice and other tiny shrimp-like creatures
- long, thin snouts
- thin trunks, hard rings
- thin tails
- small fins for steering
- eyes can move in different directions at the same time

Weedy Sea Dragons

- red, purple, and yellow bodies
- grow up to 18 inches long
- lives among bright colored sponges deep in the water

Sea dragons are fun to watch but difficult to find. They are constantly playing a game of hide and seek with people. Sea dragons call the waters off the coast of Australia home. They swim between the plants and sponges growing in the water. They blend into these other living things. This makes the sea dragons hard to spot. This ability to blend in is the sea dragon's main form of defense. For years, divers caught sea dragons to keep as pets. They captured so many, the number of sea dragons living freely dropped greatly. The sea dragons needed help. The government passed laws to protect the sea dragons. The laws stop people from removing the creatures. They want future generations to watch the sea dragons. They want the sea dragons to live there forever.

36. What is one way a   4R1c Inf
    weedy sea dragon looks
    different from a leafy sea
    dragon?

    A. A weedy sea dragon has a thin
       tail.

    B. A weedy sea dragon has two
       eyes.

    C. A weedy sea dragon can have
       a purple body.

    D. A weedy sea dragon grows up
       to 14 inches long.

37. How do leafy sea   4R1g Inf
    dragons hide between
    plants?

    A. The government passed laws
       to give them hiding places.

    B. Their long snouts help them
       dig hiding places into the
       sand.

    C. The color and shape of their
       bodies help them look like the
       plants.

    D. The rings on the trunks of
       their bodies look like the rings
       in a tree trunk.

38. Sea dragons can steer   4R1c Inf
    themselves by using
    their

    A. fins.

    B. eyes.

    C. tails.

    D. noses.

39. The root word of   4R3c
    defensive is *defend*,
    meaning

    A. to swim in deep water.

    B. to drive away danger.

    C. to pretend to be something
       else.

    D. to play in an interesting game.

40. What does the word *gener-*   4R3b
    ations mean in the sen-
    tence below?

    They want future generations to
    watch the sea dragons.

    A. eggs that will hatch sea
    dragons some day

    B. divers who catch woody and
       leafy sea dragons

    C. groups of people born around
       the same time

    D. sets of colorful water plants
       and sponges

Tea Time

Yoko measured tea leaves into the strainer and lowered it into the teapot. Then, she poured steaming water over the leaves. As the tea brewed, Yoko prepared the tray. First, she smoothed a lace cloth over the polished surface. Then, she placed a teacup and saucer on the tray and balanced a spoon along the saucer's rim. Next, she selected three pastries and placed them in a triangle on a plate. Grandmother insisted on three pastries—never two, never four—always three. Yoko placed the plate and checked the time. Grandmother would be displeased if the tea wasn't perfectly brewed. The time allowed Yoko to pull a linen napkin from the drawer. She pressed perfect pleats into the cloth, folded it, and placed the linen fan on the tray. Yoko checked the clock again. She needed to work quickly. Yoko sliced lemon wedges and placed three wedges on a plate on the tray. Yoko glanced at the clock. It was time to remove the tea leaves. She pulled the strainer out of the pot like a pail from a well. Yoko covered the pot and transferred it to the tray. Yoko studied the tray. The pastries were in the center and the napkin was in the twelve o'clock position. Yoko saw the teacup at two o'clock and the lemon wedges at three. The teapot stood boldly at the ten o'clock position. Yoko congratulated herself. She doubted Grandmother would praise her efforts, but she felt proud of her work.

41. How does Yoko feel about her grandmother?   4R1b Lit

    A. She wants to please her.

    B. She wants to be like her.

    C. She enjoys laughing with her grandmother.

    D. She is grateful for her grand-mother's kind words.

42. Which is an example of a simile?   4R1d Lit

    A. placed them in a triangle

    B. pressed perfect pleats

    C. like a pail from a well

    D. teapot stood boldly

43. It seems as though Yoko's grandmother is very demanding. What information in the story shows this? 4R1f Lit

A. As the tea brewed, Yoko prepared the tray.

B. Grandmother insisted on three pastries.

C. She needed to work quickly.

D. Yoko sliced lemon wedges.

44. Why does Yoko keep checking the time? 4R1b Lit

A. She is waiting for Grandmother to come over for tea.

B. She knows the tea has to brew for a certain number of minutes.

C. She is trying to remember where each item belongs on the tray.

D. She is trying to prepare the tea tray faster than Grandmother could.

45. The word *displeased* means 4R3e

A. "to not be happy."

B. "to be very happy."

C. "to later be happy."

D. "to be happy again."

Square Dancing

The roots of square dancing are in Europe. However, Americans added a twist to the art form—the caller. What does a caller do? The caller directs traffic on the dance floor. He calls a series of steps that dancers follow in the order given. A caller keeps dancers moving in time with each other and flowing from spot to spot. A new dancer might not recognize the caller's language. Steps have names like, "Cut a diamond. Fill a boat." The caller must realize the dancers' experience levels. Then, he can explain the steps as needed and keep the dancers moving.

46. What does the word *roots* 4R3h
    mean in this sentence?

    The roots of square dancing roots
    are in Europe.

    A. a set of cheers

    B. the act of hunting

    C. lower part of a plant or tooth

    D. a source or beginning of
       something

47. The information in the 4R1d Inf
    paragraph is organized
    in

    A. time order.

    B. cause and effect order.

    C. question and answer order.

    D. problem and solution order.

48. What is the topic sen- 4R2b Inf
    tence of the paragraph?

    A. Square dancing's roots are in
       Europe.

    B. What does a caller do?

    C. Steps have names like, "Cut a
       diamond. Fill a boat."

    D. Then, he can explain the steps
       as needed and keep the danc-
       ers moving.

49. What does a caller do if 4R1e Inf
    he knows there are
    many new dancers on the floor?

    A. makes the dances shorter

    B. explains the names of the
       steps

    C. separates the new and old
       dancers

    D. calls the steps without any
       music

50. How did Americans 4R1a Inf
    change the dance form?

    A. They added a caller.

    B. They changed the steps'
       names.

    C. They changed the dance floor.

    D. They put the dancers in
       squares.

Mastering the Georgia 4th Grade CRCT in Reading

Practice Test 2

The purpose of this practice test is to measure your knowledge in reading comprehension. This practice test is based on the Georgia Performance Standards for reading and adheres to the sample question format provided by the Georgia Department of Education.

General Directions:

1. Read all directions carefully.

2. Read each question or sample. Then choose the best answer.

3. Choose only one answer for each question. If you change an answer, be sure to erase your original answer completely.

Section 1

Two Frogs

Two frogs lived far apart. One frog, Felicity, lived on a tree branch beside the sea. The other frog, Ferdinand, lived under a rock next to a river.

One day, a salamander said to Felicity, "Aren't you tired of staring at the same old sea? I know a place where water sparkles like diamonds."

Felicity admitted that she was tired of the sea. By the time she'd had dinner, she knew she had to see the sparkling diamond water.

Meanwhile, Ferdinand was sitting by his river when a bird chirped, "Aren't you tired of staring at the same tiny stream? I know a place where water stretches as far as you can see."

Before the birds could flutter a feather, Ferdinand asked them how to find the big body of water.

At sunrise, both frogs began their long hops away from home. Felicity hurried as fast as she could. She reached the top of a huge hill and found some shade to rest in. Ferdinand scaled the hill shortly after her. He also wanted to get out of the sun. He happened to choose the same shade as Felicity.

"I'm on my way to visit a new place. How about you?" asked Ferdinand.

"That sounds great! I'm also off to see something new," Felicity replied.

The frogs agreed that both of their journeys were going well. They also agreed that the hill was too large to see past. Felicity had an idea.

"Hop onto my shoulders and see what you can see," she said.

Ferdinand hopped up and looked into the distance. He exclaimed, "It's beautiful! The water sparkles like diamonds!"

He thanked Felicity for her help and hopped away in a hurry. Felicity guessed Ferdinand must have liked what he saw. Realizing he had hopped in the same direction from which he'd come, Felicity decided to take a look back. She gasped at the sight of water as far as she could see. It was so beautiful! She had lived by the sea all her life, but she had never seen it from the top of a hill. She hopped home. She was eager to find a new tree branch to live in—one that wasn't so close to the ground.

1. The first frog and the 4R1b Lit
   second frog were

   A. friends.

   B. brothers.

   C. strangers.

   D. neighbors.

2. Who is telling the story? 4R1c Lit

   A. the birds

   B. a narrator

   C. the first frog

   D. the second frog

3. Which is a simile? 4R1d Lit

   A. the endless sea

   B. water sparkles like diamonds

   C. liked what he saw

   D. the same old sea

4. What MOST likely 4R1f Lit
   would Ferdinand have
   done if he had looked in the right
   direction?

   A. He would have stayed on the hill.

   B. He would have immediately gone home.

   C. He would have finished his journey.

   D. He would have followed Felicity.

5. What lesson is found in 4R1h Lit
   the story?

   A. It can be good to look at things from a new angle.

   B. It is not easy to make a new friend.

   C. Don't get your ideas from others.

   D. Be prepared for every problem.

Hat History

Do you wear a hat or cap when you go out? If so, you are following in the footsteps of your ancestors. Many historians believe head coverings trace back as far as the cave dwellers. These early hats were not fashion statements. They were a way of protecting heads from unpleasant weather. However, by ancient times, hats came to symbolize a person's rank in life. Ancient Greeks and Romans made felt from sheep's wool. They used the wool to make a simple skull cap. The cap could only be worn by free men. When a Greek or Roman slave was given his freedom, he was presented with one of these "liberty caps."

By the 1600s, hats also showed the man's sense of style. In addition to felt, hats were made of fur or straw. The close fitting caps were replaced by hats with crowns as high as seven inches. Over time, the height of the crown and width of the brim changed. Men were always looking for a practical but stylish head covering.

From early time, women kept their heads covered in public. Veils, scarves, hoods, and simple caps served that purpose. When they did begin wearing hats, the hat designs were based on men's hats. In the late 1600s, this changed. Hat makers began making styles just for women. This was a great time for women. Women's hats became an important part of fashion.

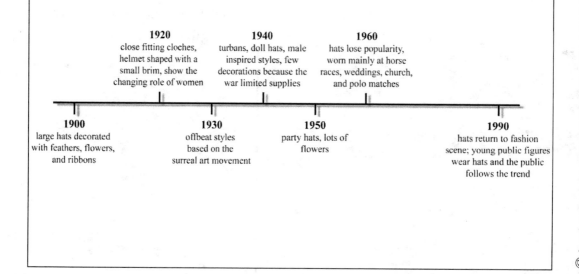

	1920		1940		1960	
	close fitting cloches, helmet shaped with a small brim, show the changing role of women		turbans, doll hats, male inspired styles, few decorations because the war limited supplies		hats lose popularity, worn mainly at horse races, weddings, church, and polo matches	
1900		**1930**		**1950**		**1990**
large hats decorated with feathers, flowers, and ribbons		offbeat styles based on the surreal art movement		party hats, lots of flowers		hats return to fashion scene; young public figures wear hats and the public follows the trend

6. Which is the topic sentence of paragraph 2? 4R1b Inf

   A. By the 1600s, hats also showed the man's sense of style.

   B. In addition to felt, hats were made of fur or straw.

   C. Over time, the height of the crown and width of the brim changed.

   D. Men were always looking for a practical but stylish head covering.

7. How did women's hats change in the 1940s? 4R1c Inf

   A. They had much larger brims.

   B. They had more flowers on them.

   C. They had fewer decorations on them.

   D. They had a smaller brim and a helmet shape.

8. Which is the best summary of paragraph 1? 4R1f Inf

   A. If you wear hats, you are like people who lived a long time ago.

   B. There would not be a history of hats if not for the sheep's wool.

   C. Men have always worn hats or caps, but the reasons for wearing them changed over time.

   D. In Ancient Greece and Rome, you could tell if a man was free by the liberty cap he wore.

9. Which sentence is an opinion? 4R1h Inf

   A. Ancient Greeks and Romans made felt from sheep's wool.

   B. In addition to felt, hats were made of fur or straw.

   C. In the late 1600s, this changed.

   D. This was a great time for women.

10. As it is used in the passage, the word *crown* means 4R3h

    A. "a reward."

    B. "a wreath."

    C. "a gold or silver British coin."

    D. "the highest point of something."

The Parboiled Detectives

"It was the vegetables!" accused the lumpy lad.

"I tried to tell my mother they were very, very bad.

Here we sat enjoying a hot and healthy meal,

When my dear sweet mother began to spin and reel."

The farmer gathered the suspects around the kitchen table.

"Which of you has done this to my darling wife Mabel?

Who made this lovely lady flush and faint and fall?

I want the one who did this or I will take you all."

"Let us work together," begged the iceberg and romaine,

As the angry farmer tossed them above the kitchen drain.

"I wasn't stalking her!" cried the crisp, green celery.

"So, please keep that paring knife far away from me!"

"Let's dip a little further, you are a reasonable bloke,

We'll get to the heart of this," prevailed the artichoke.

But, the farmer was losing patience; his face was turning red,

The lady had done her fainting before the hungry farmer was fed.

The tomato saw an opening and hopped onto the floor.

"I'm not a veggie," he said, rolling out the door.

"Halt!" yelled the farmer in red-hot pursuit.

"You are a suspect – vegetable or fruit."

They raced through the garden, row after row,

'Till the angry farmer tripped on the garden hoe.

"That's it!" declared the farmer, rubbing his bumpy head.

He started pulling veggies from their safe and comfy bed.

The vegetables started to panic, not knowing what to do,

To keep themselves from becoming a pot of veggie stew.

Until the brave potato shouted above the others' cries,

"The whole thing happened right before this tater's eyes."

A gasp escaped from the veggies—red, yellow and green.

Just what would the spud say his many eyes had seen?

"It wasn't the asparagus, the beets, or watercress,

It was the lad who caused the lady to be in such distress."

"It's true!" declared the corncob. "I heard it with my own ears.
The lady is quite lucky she didn't drown in her own tears.
She tried to feed him the onion, the spinach, and the pea.
She offered him every vegetable, working from A to Z.
No matter what she offered to her picky, stubborn son,
The answer stayed the same, 'No thanks. I'll have none.'
If only he had tasted the red peppers or bokchoy,
The farmer would be dining with his wife and little boy."

11. Which pair of words rhymes? 4R1i Lit

   A. lad, meal

   B. drain, celery

   C. floor, door

   D. hoe, head

12. Which is an example of alliteration? 4R1i Lit

   A. Who made this lovely lady flush and faint and fall?

   B. So, please keep that paring knife far away from me!

   C. But, the farmer was losing patience; his face was turning red,

   D. The tomato saw an opening and hopped down on the floor.

13. Read the following line from the poem. 4R1d Lit
Until the brave potato shouted above the others' cries,

This is an example of

   A. simile.

   B. metaphor.

   C. assonance.

   D. personification.

14. Why did the farmer's wife faint? 4R1b Lit

   A. Her son refused to eat any vegetables.

   B. She had been cooking over a hot stove.

   C. The farmer arrived home late for dinner.

   D. She had never before seen vegetables talk.

15. The word *distress* means 4R3a

   A. "a sleepy state."

   B. "a big surprise."

   C. "a great suffering."

   D. "a vegetable garden."

Wendy Mass

Every morning, millions of people in New Jersey battle traffic. They board buses or trains or drive cars on the crowded roadways. They are all hurrying off to work. New Jersey native Wendy Mass is glad she is not one of them. Mass is the author of sixteen books for children and young adults. On most days, she only has to commute as far as her living room sofa.

Freedom from the traffic is a great perk of Mass's career choice, but it isn't why she writes. Mass developed a love for books early in life. She loved being read to, and she loved reading. When she graduated from college, a writing career seemed like a natural choice. She started by writing book reviews, newspaper articles, and short stories. The experiences helped her write her first novel. It was never published, but by then, she was hooked on the idea of writing for children and teens. It took eight years of trying before her first book was published.

Like many other writers, Mass has found a writing process that works for her. She starts by researching her topic. She can do some of the research at home using the Internet. However, Mass also makes frequent trips to libraries. She loves doing research so much that she sometimes has a hard time stopping to start writing. When she does begin to write, she starts with pen and paper. Mass writes a very detailed outline of her story in a notebook. When she is happy with the outline, she switches to her laptop. She sets a goal for the number of pages she wants to write in a day. She may not always meet her goal, but she knows it's important to have one.

When she isn't writing books, Mass speaks to groups and autographs books. She works on her Web site (wendymass.com) and her blog to let her fans know what is new. Mass has adapted her writing routine over time. She is the mother of two-year-old twins. It's hard to find quiet writing time at home with two active toddlers. So, she often goes to the library to write when she has a deadline to meet. Being able to go with the flow of her life has brought Mass success in both fiction and nonfiction writing. Her "never give up" attitude has earned her many fans and kept her out of rush hour traffic.

16. Today, Mass mainly writes   4R1a Inf

   A. short stories.

   B. book reviews.

   C. newspaper articles.

   D. books for teens and children.

17. Paragraph 3 is organized in   4R1d Inf

   A. process order.

   B. cause and effect order.

   C. problem/solution order.

   D. compare and contrast order.

18. Why does the author include Mass's Web site address in the passage?   4LSV2a

   A. to show Mass is a real person

   B. to show where Mass does her research

   C. to give readers a way to learn more about Mass

   D. to explain why Mass has less time for writing books

19. Why does the author describe Mass as a "never give up" person?   4R1g Inf

   A. She is the mother of two active children.

   B. She decided to become a writer when she was a child.

   C. She worked for eight years before selling her first book.

   D. She loves researching so much that she never wants to stop.

20. The root word *graph* means *write*. The word *autograph* means   4R3c

   A. "to read many books."

   B. "to sell pens and paper."

   C. "to sign one's own name."

   D. "to copy someone's work."

Zip!

Jake was relying on his gut as much as his feet to win the race. It was his gut that told him to go left at the fork in the road. It was his gut that told him to continue as he struggled up the steep hill. It was his gut that told him spotting two race officials, standing on the platform before him, meant trouble. The taller guy said, "You're the first person to make it this far. Of course, everyone else might have gone the other way, but that route is much longer. We'll put you in the harness; you'll step off the platform, and glide down in two minutes flat. Folks on the other route have to run down. This zip line will give you a thirty minute advantage."

Jake's legs were two strands of cooked spaghetti. He felt his stomach drop to his knees as he slipped into the harness. "Just don't look down," he thought, as he shuffled to the platform's edge. Jake breathed deeply and stepped back away from the edge. He thought about the time needed to run back to the fork in the road and run the other route. It most certainly would mean defeat. He stepped forward again, closed his eyes, and started soaring down the wire.

About the author

The author loves nature, facing challenges, and trying new things. But, her fear of heights keeps her from cliff diving, bungee jumping, and riding those giant slides in amusement parks!

21. The sentence, "Jake's 4R1d Lit
    legs were two strands of
    cooked spaghetti." is an example
    of

    A. simile.

    B. metaphor.

    C. assonance.

    D. personification.

22. What best describes 4R1f Lit
    Jake?

    A. set on winning

    B. too lazy to run

    C. happy with his choices

    D. excited about the zip line

23. How are Jake and the 4R1g Lit
    author alike?

    A. They both love nature.

    B. They both rode a zip line.

    C. They are both afraid of
       heights.

    D. They are both running in a
       race.

24. Who is telling the 4R1c Lit
    story?

    A. Jake

    B. the narrator

    C. another runner

    D. a race official

25. The antonym of *defeat* is 4R3i

    A. *loss.*

    B. *trying.*

    C. *sadness.*

    D. *victory.*

Section 2

onceuponatime.com

Our Shop

Fairytales

Folktales

History

Write Your
Own Ending

Character
Match

Once upon a Time...

Welcome! Our goal is to bring fairytales, folktales, and fun to you. Explore our site to learn about the rich history of storytelling. Read classic fairytales and folktales from around the world. Play games based on famous favorite characters, or write your own ending to our tales. Then, stop by our online shop to discover the many treasures it holds. We offer the best selection of books, audio tapes, and DVDs. We sell a wide variety of games and costumes. We even have stage settings so you can perform your own fairytale plays at home.

26. Where would you find a free game on the Web site? 4LSV2c

A. History

B. Our Shop

C. Fairytales

D. Character Match

27. Why does the author use the word *treasures* to describe the things sold in the shop? 4LSV2b

A. The things they sell are very old.

B. Storytelling has a long, rich history.

C. So readers will believe the things are worth buying.

D. Fairytales and folktales always include a treasure.

28. Which sentence from the passage is an opinion? 4R1h Inf

A. Our goal is to bring fairytales, folktales, and fun to you.

B. Read classic fairytales and folktales from around the world.

C. We offer the best selection of books, audio tapes, and DVDs.

D. We sell a wide variety of games and costumes.

29. Which is a homophone for the word *tales*? 4R3i

A. facts

B. tails

C. heads

D. stories

30. Read the following sentence from the passage. 4R3b

We even have stage settings so you can perform your own fairytale plays at home.

In this sentence, the word *perform* means

A. "to act."

B. "to buy."

C. "to paint."

D. "to watch."

The Case of the Bushy-Tailed Bandit

"Kevin, go claim our spot," Gramps said, as soon as my feet touched the gravel parking lot.

I jogged ahead to our favorite picnic table in the clearing between the oak trees. Mom loved the perfect blend of sun and shade there, while Gramps and I appreciated its lakeside location. As I reached the clearing, two squirrels scurried up one of the oak trees. I don't know why Gramps always sends me ahead, since I've never seen anyone anywhere near our spot. It seemed like the perfect picnic place was known only by us and, of course, the squirrels.

When Mom and Gramps arrived they placed the basket and the thermos of lemonade on the table. Then, Mom relaxed under a tree with a book, while Gramps and I headed to the lake. We were enjoying our monthly rock skipping contest when Mom joined us. "Are you gentlemen hungry yet?" she asked.

We hurried back to the clearing, with my mouth watering at the thought of that picnic basket. Today, Gramps had packed it, so I knew it held peanut butter and honey sandwiches, chips, and cookies. When Mom packed lunch, it was a whole different menu: salad, fruit, and whole wheat bread. When we reached the table, I flung open the picnic basket. My jaw dropped like a drawbridge. The sandwiches were missing!

Disappointed, I asked, "Gramps, are you sure you packed the sandwiches in the basket?"

"I'm sure," Gramps answered. "I never forget food."

I looked around the table and under the table, but there wasn't a sandwich in sight. I stood on a tree stump and slowly turned, looking in every direction. I turned my attention to Mom. "Mom," I said. "You don't care for peanut butter and honey sandwiches. Did you remove them from the basket?"

Mom shook her head. "It's true, I prefer a healthier lunch, and cookies and chips aren't my idea of a healthy lunch."

She had a point, but I was out of suspects. I was also so hungry; I was imagining the faint scent of peanut butter in the air. Then, a plastic bag floated down from the sky. I looked up and discovered the bushy-tailed bandits. Three squirrels were sitting on a branch enjoying our meal. Each had a sandwich between its front paws. The extras were wedged between the branch and the trunk. I guess our secret picnic place is not so secret after all.

31. Which sentence is an example of foreshadowing? 4R1e Lit

A. I jogged ahead to our favorite picnic table in the clearing between the oak trees.

B. It seemed like the perfect picnic place was known only by us and, of course, the squirels.

C. When we reached the table, I flung open the picnic basket.

D. Three squirrels were sitting on a branch enjoying our meal.

32. Who is telling the story? 4R1c Lit

A. Mom

B. Kevin

C. Gramps

D. narrator

33. Why did Kevin suspect Mom of taking the sandwiches? 4R1b Lit

A. She said she was not hungry.

B. She was alone with the basket.

C. She did not like the sandwiches.

D. She always played tricks on them.

34. Which sentence includes a simile? 4R1d Lit

A. As I reached the clearing, two squirrels scurried up one of the oak trees.

B. My jaw dropped like a drawbridge.

C. The sandwiches were missing!

D. I looked up and discovered the bushy-tailed bandits.

35. Use the dictionary entries to answer the question. 4R3d

cradle (v.) to hold closely

cram (v.) to pack tightly

crate (v.) to pack into a box

crease (v.) to fold with an edge

Which word can be used instead of *wedged* in the sentence: *The extras were wedged between the branch and the trunk.*

A. cradled

B. crammed

C. crated

D. creased

Sea Lions

Sea lions seem to love an audience, and audiences love sea lions. Sea lions live in or near the Pacific Ocean. Others live in zoos and aquariums. Wherever they are, sea lions always draw a crowd.

Sea lions belong to an animal group called pinnipeds. The word *pinniped* means "wing foot" or "feather foot." Their wing-like flippers at the end of their limbs help them swim in the water. Sea lions are fast swimmers. If needed, they swim as fast as twenty-five miles per hour. While their front flippers help them in the water, their rear flippers help them on land. The hind flippers can rotate or turn, helping the sea lion scoot along rocky ridges or sandy beaches. Sea lions can even use their flippers to body surf on breaking waves!

Sea lions also have sleek bodies, perfect for diving. They can dive as deep as six hundred feet into the water. This is very helpful since they fish for their dinner. When a sea lion dives into the water its nostrils seal shut. It never has to worry about water going up its snout!

Perhaps one reason people love sea lions is their dog-like faces. They have dark eyes and excellent vision. However, they are unable to see colors. They have small ear flaps on each side of their heads and good hearing. On their pointed snouts, they have long sensitive whiskers. The whiskers are loosely attached to the upper lip. A sea lion's whiskers twist and move with the water currents. This makes it possible for a sea lion to feel food swimming by before it seeing it.

As you can probably guess from its name, a sea lion can roar. It also can bark or honk. As a matter of fact, one way people find sea lions living freely is too listen for those sounds. Sea lions are very social animals. They live in large groups or colonies. When a colony starts roaring, barking, and honking, they are very loud! People in search of sea lions can follow the noise to find the colony.

People love watching sea lions in their day-to-day activities. They watch them swim, dive, walk, rest, and "talk." Sea lions are also very intelligent. Trainers teach them to perform these actions on cue. Whether the sea lions live in the ocean or in a zoo, they always draw a crowd of fans.

36. Because the sea lion's whiskers are loose, 4R1e Inf

   A. they are above the lip.

   B. they fall in the water.

   C. they feel fish coming near.

   D. they make eating difficult.

37. Why don't sea lions take in water when they dive? 4R1e Inf

   A. because their nostrils seal shut

   B. because they are good swimmers

   C. because they have a dog-like face

   D. because they dive deep into the water

38. Sea lions have very good vision, but they can't see 4R1a Inf

   A. colors.

   B. people.

   C. things on land.

   D. things in water.

39. What is the most important idea in paragraph 5? 4R1f Inf

   A. Sea lions live in colonies.

   B. Sea lions are very social.

   C. Sea lions make loud noises.

   D. Sea lions can roar like a lion.

The following question is not about the passage.

40. The word *remix* means 4R3e

   A. "to mix again."

   B. "to mix less."

   C. "to mix perfectly."

   D. "to mix lightly."

The Grasshopper That Wouldn't Hop

There once lived a grasshopper that refused to learn how to hop. When the other grasshoppers went to hopping classes, he stayed home. His mother begged him to go, and his father warned that a grasshopper that couldn't hop faced many dangers. But, the lazy grasshopper always answered, "Why should I learn to hop? I can walk wherever I want to go. I can eat the sweet grass that grows near the ground and the crunchy carrots that grow in the ground. I do not need to hop!"

One day, the lazy grasshopper and his friends decided to visit a nearby farm. The lazy grasshopper walked as quickly as possible, but he couldn't keep up with the others. "Wait for me!" he shouted.

"Hop!" they shouted back.

But, the lazy grasshopper did not know how to hop. By the time he reached the farm, his friends were already eating the tall stalks of corn that grew in the field. "I'm hungry," he complained.

The other grasshoppers said, "Eat some corn."

The lazy grasshopper answered, "How can I eat plants up there, when I'm down here?"

He hoped someone would offer to bring him some food.

Instead, the grasshoppers said, "Hop!"

But, the lazy grasshopper did know how to hop. Before long, he heard boots pounding against the soil like claps of thunder. The lazy grasshopper shouted, "Farmer!"

"Hop for your life!" shouted the other grasshoppers, as they hopped to safety. But, the lazy grasshopper did not know how to hop.

41. What lesson is in the story? 4R1h Lit

A. Always stay close to home.

B. Never eat your neighbor's food.

C. Learn today what you may need tomorrow.

D. Don't ask others to do what you won't do yourself.

42. Why did the author write, "...his father warned that a grasshopper that couldn't hop faced many dangers?" 4R1e Lit

A. to show the grasshopper had a family

B. to hint at the trouble that would happen later

C. to explain that most grass-hoppers hop

D. to show that his father was very smart

43. What MOST likely happens next to the lazy grasshopper? 4R1f Lit

A. He outruns the farmer.

B. He takes hopping classes.

C. He gets caught by the farmer.

D. He helps the other grass-hoppers.

44. Why didn't the lazy grasshopper take hop-ping classes? 4R1b Lit

A. Hopping hurt his legs.

B. He was too young to go.

C. He did not like the other young grasshoppers.

D. He did not see any reason to learn how to hop.

45. Who is telling the story? 4R1c Lit

A. a narrator

B. the farmer

C. the lazy grasshopper

D. the grasshopper's friends

Spy Secrets

There were many spies at work during the American Revolution. Both sides needed spies to pass messages. The spies had clever ways of doing this. They used secret codes, invisible ink, and blind drops. These steps kept the information safe.

Many different secret codes were used. Most used letters or numbers in place of other letters or words. No one could read the message without the key to the code. One secret code used a dictionary. The writer looked up the word in the dictionary. They counted how many words came before it on the page. Then, the writer replaced the word in their letter with the page and placement numbers.

Another spy trick was writing with invisible ink. One spy wrote a secret message between lines of a letter. The person who received the letter held it over a flame. The heat made the secret message appear.

Blind drops were also used. A blind drop is a place two people agree upon, like a hollow tree. One person leaves the message there, and another person picks it up. Sometimes, the blind drop was so tiny it could fit in the palm of your hand. The spy cut the message into small strips. The strips were stuffed into a small hollow silver ball. People could easily pass the ball to someone without being seen. If someone stopped the messenger, he or she could hide or swallow the silver ball. The spies never wanted their enemy to see the secret messages.

46. Which is the topic sen- 4R1b Inf
tence of paragraph 3?

A. Another spy trick was writing with invisible ink.

B. One spy wrote a secret message between lines of a letter.

C. The person who received the letter held it over a flame.

D. The heat made the secret message appear.

Read the following sentence 4R3h from the passage.

> No one could read the message without the key to the code.

47. Which sentence uses the word *key* in the same way it is used in the passage?

A. Robin placed her *key* in the lock.

B. I struck the wrong *key* on the piano.

C. Dan wrote the *key* ideas from the book on the board.

D. I used the *key* to understand the pictures on the map.

48. The blind drop balls 4R1e Inf could be passed without being seen because

A. they were tiny.

B. they were silver.

C. they were swallowed.

D. they held strips of paper.

49. Paragraph 2 is organized 4R1d Inf in

A. time order.

B. process order.

C. problem/solution order.

D. compare/contrast order.

50. Which word is a synonym 4R3i for *clever*?

A. dull

B. silly

C. smart

D. difficult

T

V

W